BRIGHT ROMANTIC ADVENTURES

BRIGHT ROMANTIC ADVENTURES

MAIRI COLME

THE REGENCY PUBLISHERS

ISBN: 978-1-960113-54-2   (Paperback Edition)
ISBN: 978-1-960113-55-9   (Hardcover Edition)
ISBN: 978-1-960113-53-5   (E-book Edition)

Book Ordering Information

The Regency Publishers, International
7 Bell Yard London WO2A2JR

info@theregencypublishers.com
www.theregencypublishers.international
+44 20 8133 0466

Printed in the United States of America

CONTENTS

FURTHER ADVENTURES OF EMILY

Jenny my own, Jenny my love

A Historical Romance

CHAPTER 1

Through the Forest

HE CAME CRASHING through the forest. The tangled trees gave way before him, lashing his legs and whipping at his face. It was an ancient forest, one of those as ancient as the world itself. Somerled suspended his movement for just a moment, long enough to check that the soldiers were still chasing their quarry. Yes, he could hear their fierce cries and angry feet. Now the aim was, not to avoid capture, but to let himself be caught - -

He had to remind himself, to actively bring to mind the plan, his hastily concocted plot for putting things right. But it was easier to create an idealistic plan in the cool of calmness, than it was to stick to it in the heat of action. Suddenly the trees stopped, and he was standing on the edge of rock, which plunged precipitously down. He veered across to the right, through more trees.

This seemed like virgin forest, yet he suddenly found himself on a track. What had made this downward path he couldn't conceive, but it was muddy. He became aware of the bright morning sun, lancing through all the leaves. It had recently rained, he noted, for the light shone on all the little waterdrops on leaves and blades of grass, so that they glittered like scattered jewels. It was such a vision of brightness and freshness.

"God, I'd hate to leave this world," he thought, "sometimes it's like heaven."

Somerled wondered why he hadn't noticed the water before, the rainfall which had left every ounce of the wood, every recess of it, either shining or treacherously slippy. Why had he not noticed it as he had climbed over the wall of the fort, his fingernails scratching on the stone, before he plummeted into the row of trees, and held his breath to see if he was followed? Why hadn't he been aware of the early morning dampness, due to the rain-shower just missed, as he stood and hearkened for the hue and cry? Why on earth was it that not until now, when his life was maybe short in front of him, that he been awake to the world's bright beauty?

But the water also made the going treacherous underfoot. Suddenly the heel of his boots rutched forward on the waterlogged track, and he slipped down and down, truly crashing now down the slope, down the steep valley toward the burn which was churning excitedly below.

He stopped when there was no further to go, because he landed in the water. He stood up. "How unpleasant!" he remarked, feeling his wet breeches. This morning was very strange, he reflected, because here he was, pursued and in danger on what could be the last morning of his life, yet he had never looked more intensely at the sparking beauty of the world around him, or felt more vividly the experience of physical discomfort.

"Maybe this is the last morning of my life," he wryly remarked as he got up. Maybe the Almighty was telling him something. What though?

The burn was rushing quite deep in front of him, - too deep; he couldn't ford it at this spot. He waded forward for a bit along the bank. Seeing the track had led down here, maybe there was some way of crossing. He waded in shallow water along the edge for a while, intently perusing the shape and size of the stones which looked glazed and wet.

What on earth was the matter with him? He was being pursued by the Jacobites' enemies, those despised redcoats, in the pay of the hated George, who was not and never could be the right and true king of Scotland, - bonny Scotland, his homeland, - and all he could do was obsess about the brightness of seeing jewels in the wood and the lovely shapeliness of stones!

"What is this?" he said aloud. Was it the last-minute awarenesses of a man condemned to die? Was it because his mind couldn't get itself around the plan, the urgency of putting things right? Maybe he wasn't going to live; that was the point. Maybe when the soldiers finally caught up with him, they would simply and mercilessly kill him. That would certainly scupper his plan.

He came round the corner, where the burn suddenly took a right-angled turn. And before him was a tiny little stone bridge, its stones all higgledy-piggledy, looking quite new. He wasn't surprised, for he half expected it. Suddenly his awareness of the world around him seemed to have taken a fairy-tale turn. It just seemed a magical bridge in what was an unreal landscape.

He'd forgotten the soldiers! Were they still following him? His foot was on the bridge, before he remembered them. Suddenly he didn't care. He stood there transfixed by the toss of the turbulent water as it rushed under the arch of the bridge; he sensed the elemental power of it. He stood with a feeling like intoxication.

"Why don't I end the whole sorry mess?" This thought popped into his mind unbidden. He desired just to rest, to sleep, from all the torment of his young life. He was only twenty- eight years of age, and yet these years weighed so heavily on him. He had in so short a time made a mess of the young lives surrounding him. He so much wanted to be like his father; idealistically and unflinchingly fighting for a cause, holding in honour above all the values of integrity, trueness to friendship, faithfulness to allies and family in the good old clan way. Yet it had all come unstuck; he himself had come unstuck. He had failed in his own deepest ideals.

"Why go on?" Why not just let himself be swept away in the rush of water, just to lay it all down, to let the Almighty take care of it? And in perhaps the way only the Almighty can? Whilst he with his own little machinations was trying to put things right, to atone, to earn forgiveness for betrayal, for death? Yes, to be one with the water, as it plunged over the rocks under the bridge - -

Yet above the roar of the water he heard the noise of broken branches, now very near. He closed his eyes. His consciousness was awake, so aware, that he could sense with a preternatural intensity the breaking of the twigs underfoot and the hot breath of the chasing soldiers pluming in the early atmosphere of the pristine wood. He sensed their impetuous presence and his own impending capture. And he sensed too the beauty of all of nature around him- the sparklingness of the wet wood, the smoothness of the stones, the wildness of the rushing water - -

It all had meaning, he thought. Seeing his awareness had expanded with such delicious intensity, maybe this was the end for him. He relaxed his muscles, and just stood, silent and still, on the bridge. He had run far enough to convince them that he had secrets to tell, truth that could be prized from him. He should stop running now.

With his eyes closed, he thought for a fleeting moment of that image which seemed to flit around his dream-world and his waking hours. He sensed the long gorgeous black hair entangled in his hands, as he buried his head deep in Jenny's tresses. And again that image of a rainbow arched in the spray of a plummeting waterfall. Was it a memory he couldn't place, or an augury of something to come? "Jenny his own, Jenny his love, Jenny who would never forgive him."

CHAPTER 2

On the Floor

SOMETHING CHIMED INTO his consciousness, like the tolling of a bell, as he lay with demolished morale on the prison floor. "You will rue the day, you will rue the day!" It was his mother's voice. He thought she was being unduly emotional as she stood by the fire stirring the skillet. But then again she was credited with a gift of second sight. And it was the day he had first laid eyes on Jenny.

He had laughed at the time over her silliness; it had been occasioned by some slight altercation, the subject of which he couldn't now recall. He only remembered the words, those high-pitched motherly words whose utterance were designed to shepherd and guide. It had made him throw his head back with a glad laugh, and proclaim he was setting off over the ben to walk to his friend's house, - his best and only friend Malcolm.

His mother and himself, his father having passed away, lived on a croft far from the beaten track, down by the loch of Glen Etive. They had a good life, though a hard one, for there was much work to be done on a croft. He himself did all the farming work these days, tilling the soil and urging crops to grow, and tending his small herd of cattle, which he occasionally had to take to market down the drover's roads. He had been to the big towns though he didn't like them, preferring this quiet life with his mother. After the strong and glad days of her youth, spent on the land with Somerled's father, she had relinquished her hold on the hard work, and fallen back into tending the house, sewing and mending, and forever cooking. She did make some money though, with her spinning and loom-work. Somerled was very fond of his mother, and understood all her moods.

So there she was on this bright summer's morning, saying unusually for her, "you will rue the day!" They had been talking of his plans,- he was always making plans- for getting together with Malcolm on some wild adventure, and his mother had not been best pleased with the thought of his leaving her. Again the memory of their exact point of difference escaped him, as he lay there on the prison floor. Again now he was making plans for getting out of the mess which had all begun the particular June morning when he walked out of his mother's door and off into bright sunlight up the glen.

One of his favourite sights was Ben More. It seemed elemental, standing there like a prayer, connected with the very roots of the earth, every day in silent witness to the turning of the seasons and the whirling of the night-sky of stars. He climbed it so often, standing on its very peak, that it had become a part of him, an essential element in his own consciousness. He didn't climb it this day; he didn't feel like the challenge. He just walked with a will up the grassy sides of the glen, a solitary figure in the large dominating landscape.

It always made him feel hungry, striding across the mountain-sides like this; as if some little area in his stomach objected to not having a bowl of steaming porridge before him that instant. Yes, it made him curiously hungry and strangely solitary. He felt he was in need of something which he couldn't quite put his finger on, - comfort, warmth, companionship maybe. But he was on the way to see his best-beloved companion, the friend who had remained true to him throughout his boyhood, - Malcolm the noble and true, the brave young man with a good head on his shoulders, who was generous, and kind, and faithful. And Somerled admired these qualities; braveness and intelligence, certainly, but also he admired that finer quality of faithfulness and trueness which he couldn't quite put his finger on. For the words seemed inadequate for the soul-quality; he just knew that he could rely on Malcolm, could entrust his life to this friendship. So freely and frankly he had offered his own friendship to him. He would indeed "rue the day" that anything came between them, or when he should offend their mutual trust.

So he walked through the glens, bright and free in his soul, thinking fondly of his best friend, and of his mother too, thankful for the life he led, thankful for its simplicity and purity, and just glad to be alive. Looking back he could see that was the last day he felt so happy and carefree.

Striding along thus happily, he didn't notice that the time was wearing on, the bright noon-day past, the afternoon bringing a gentler light which illuminated the heather more softly and serenely. He was unselfconscious; indeed in his youth he never used to notice the passing of time; he had the knack of living simply in the present moment. There was as yet no torment in his soul, which made consciousness of time a necessity. How innocent he then was!

Suddenly he found himself on a knoll, looking down on the steading where his friend lived. This little house at the foot of the great mountains of Glencoe was a picture to behold. Its backdrop was the huge forested slopes, which at this time of year were a deeper green than the green grass-swards in front of him; they were like the tousled mazes of hair that the mountains wore, ringing round the fierce jagged peaks. He loved this place; the serene beauty of the spot made even more dear by the time he had spent here in companionship with his friend. They talked, they read books, they gazed languidly into the magnificent landscape. They were a part of the landscape; it was in their blood.

There was sudden cry; a woman's cry. Somerled looked up, startled. It wasn't a grief-struck cry; more like a squeal of delight. He couldn't be sure.

For a moment he stood suspended from motion on the knoll, wondering what could be the cause of that cry. Then he ran pell-mell down the slope toward the steading, thinking that someone might need help; an unknown someone, someone he had never met - - All hot and breathless he was approaching the house; then suddenly he stopped, for the door had opened.

Framed in the doorway, with the soft glow of firelight behind her head, was a young woman, a beautiful young woman. She was buxom with the soft roundedness of youth, her skin very pure and pellucid, her eyes big and brown and gentle, and she had masses of curly black hair, just falling over her shoulders like a waterfall of sheer abundance.

Somerled had stopped with a sudden jolt about ten feet away, and the breath seemed to just exude from his body, as if he were all panting with some delirious desire. He breathed out, and then seemed to stop breathing, as if he had forgotten to breathe or his blood had ceased to circulate. And yet he could feel his heart beating heavily and noisily in his chest. He stood looking at her, amazed and enchanted, and she also gazed at him, - at this hot rushing youth who seemed to have fallen without breathing in a suspense in front of her. "Who are you?" they both said at the same time.

Thankfully Somerled then started to breathe again; if he had not, he wouldn't be alive to tell the tale of that first moment. It was the moment he rehearsed over and over again in his memory, as the time when he first began to live. Or did he lose his innocence and thereby begin to die? Was that the birth of both his conscience and his sin, both his guilt and his higher life?

He didn't know it at the time of course, he didn't know the impact which this moment would have on his life forever; he just knew he felt ravished as he began to breathe again, simply aware that the air came rushing into his lungs fierce and sweet.

"And why are you two just standing gawking at each other?" The familiar voice of his friend broke the spell.

"I, I heard a cry," replied Somerled, thinking his voice sounded weak and faint, when he so badly wanted to sound manly and in command.

"This is Jenny," said his friend in a comforting manner. "Jenny, Jenny" thought Somerled; how come he had so seldom heard of anyone being called that popular highland name? What would the name Jenny now mean to him?

"You look as if you've seen a ghost," Malcolm went on, "what on earth's the matter with you?"

The young man standing mesmerized at the door was jolted into awareness. "Nothing," he replied to his friend, "I'm okay."

"Jenny, meet my best friend Somerled; isn't he a handsome fellow? And he can beat anyone at the caber-tossing with his strength and skill, for all his leanness."

Jenny put out her hand, and a very soft and gentle hand it was. Somerled took it briefly, and his fingers swept against hers. How many times in the future did he rehearse that moment over and over again, wishing he could have grasped her hand for longer, and held it intently, sensing and perusing its delicious softness. But he was being watched with curiosity, so he had intentionally only brushed her hand fleetingly.

"You certainly seem in the height of being alive," said the girl sweetly, "not at all ghost-like as our friend suggests, and also a very fine and handsome fellow, and he has it right about that, no mistake."

That was the opinion the love of his life had first expressed to him,- that he was fine and handsome, and extraordinarily alive. "Alive"- what did that now mean to him, feeling half-dead on a cold stone floor, trying to expend his life putting things right? If only he could go back to that day, and live again in the way he lived up until then! But no, death had introduced itself into his life, and all he could do was struggle to somehow make his life resurgent.

So precious had that first meeting with Jenny been; for he knew he instantly loved her! And when he got home he rehearsed the moment over and over again, turning it all over in his mind before he went to sleep, - that lovely rounded figure, the clear sweetness of the voice, that face with perfect features with the large tempting eyes framed by the luscious abandonment of deep-dark hair. And always, the softness and warmth of her skin at that brief touch of her hand, which he wished he could have held longer.

It was all so sweet, so perfect, bursting his heart out of himself as he thought of it and dwelt on it time and time again, simply treasuring the moment in his memory and holding it as sacred. "Jenny his own, Jenny his love," Jenny who made him, as she herself perceived, fully alive!

CHAPTER 3

In the Court-room

THERE WAS A grating of a heavy bar and a dull thud. Somerled awoke; in an instant his eyes opened with awareness; all thoughts of Jenny fled. He waited, paused in suspense, wondering whether this would be the moment when he could give true testimony.

Suddenly the jailer was right next to him, handling him in a ruffian manner, his stinking breath right next to his cold face. And he was so cold; how long had he lain there forlornly on the prison floor, pondering thoughts of Jenny, of Malcolm, of a golden happy past? He had no idea, for he had lost all track of time; it could be anything between a day and a week, just wallowing in misery, yet lit and guided by thoughts of love and sweetness. The experience had been so intense it made him prone to believe in those wise beings called angels, who shepherd us when we are in darkness.

But he was jolted into the present, by the fierce man who stood over him, grabbing him so roughly and unceremoniously. Soldiers stood at the back of him, their faces appearing so white and well-washed, and their red uniforms so spruce and clean. "Ay we've got ye noo!" said one of them with a sort of glee, "noo ye'll spill the beans!" Something like a chill passed all over Somerled's body, so that he shivered; what was awaiting him now?

He was dragged to his feet, manacled thoroughly, and made to march out of the dank prison in front of them; they prodded him mercilessly as they went. As they came into the fresh air, Somerled breathed it in, feeling intoxicated by its freshness. He gazed up at the misty sky for a moment, with a pang of yearning for the life and freedom that he was probably by his own act sacrificing. A clear song came from a skylark, high up, beyond the reach of his eyes; "Ah to be young again, and not have these cares!"

They crossed the courtyard of the fort, and into the impressive building at the other end. Fort William was well constructed, designed for King George's troops to impress their will upon a defeated people. The Highlanders had had a chance to throw off the yoke; they had marched bravely all the way down to Derby, with their banners flying and their weapons aglow with zeal, their eyes shining with a ferocity of vision. "Victory to the Scots"! They were marching with Jacobite ideals, and intended to set up their own king in London. But they never got so far, Bonny Prince Charlie having turned back. Why such a miserable defeat after such a brave beginning? Why that terrible scene at Culloden, with all the brave show of Scotland lying slain on the field? He shuddered at the thought.

He stopped thinking of one horror, only to find a worse horror before his waking eyes; it was the General himself, sitting on the bench in what was appointed as a make-shift court-room. He flinched as he heard himself addressed: "So Sergeant Somerled Mackintosh, it's time to deal with this whole sorry business!" There was an intense silence for a moment, then the charges were read out; then a voice boomed "How do you plead?"

Although he had rehearsed the matter a thousand times in his head, Somerled found he couldn't speak. His mouth was dry, so dry, that he couldn't get his tongue to function. He was blanched white with fear and temerity. Could he really speak those words? Could he really bring judgement upon himself in order to try and exonerate his best friend, to earn forgiveness? Could forgiveness be earned anyway? There was a dreadfully long silence, such a silence that you could have heard a pin drop.

"I plead guilty!" came his strong voice. He gulped, and there was silence again.

Then the proceedings began, but he was semi-oblivious to what was transpiring in that room where they were judging Sergeant Somerled MacKintosh.

He thought only of poor Malcolm, and the distraught Jenny, and that body of Roberta hanging - - hanging limp and lifeless in the barn where he had discovered it, in that terrible moment, when he had realised he had done something cruel and unforgivable. And it had all begun when he had accused Malcolm of stealing that money - a small treasure for someone like him, - money tainted by blood. And he himself had blood on his hands - -

"If the money sent from the king's treasury was not appropriated by the late Malcolm Stuart, can you tell us in your own words what happened to it, in your own words?"

He gulped again. He valued honesty more than anything, and in a sense it was worse accusing someone else of such a crime, than it was to leave the charge at the hands of a man who was already dead and past caring. But he would do anything to gain forgiveness; and he had planned to blame himself - -

The story he told was distorted. "It was dark night that night, the forest was alive with night-time noises and there was no moon. When the rest of the men were asleep I got up, and crept to the horses. As stealthily as I could took the gold coin out of the saddle bags, and realising I needed something heavy, I stuffed them with pebbles from the stream, until they seemed bulky enough. I took the gold which I'd emptied into a casket, and then I hid it under a large rock in the glen. There was a waterfall there, and I stashed it by the side of the thunderous water, marking the place with stones. Then on my way back, I left some coins on the ground by Malcolm's body, to implicate him as the thief. It was I, I who took the money."

"This is intolerable!" thundered the general; "you were entrusted with this important duty, to bring that treasure up north, and you not only stole it, but you tried to blame it on your comrade in arms and friend! What sort of man are you?"

Malcolm blushed painfully and looked down. It wasn't the truth. But if only he could somehow restore truth by telling a lie - -

"You are not worthy of the uniform of a soldier sir! My verdict: guilty as charged!"

There was one of those silences again, then a hiss from his fellow-soldiers, then a man came up to him, a man who use do to be a friend of his, and spat on him.

The General had yet to pronounce his sentence. "You die a traitor's death, not that of a soldier," he said grimly. "Hanged, drawn and quartered, to show to others that they cannot meddle with the king's coin, nor king's justice!"

Somerled fell forward, his head in his hands; well, it was done now, and irrevocable. He had told the biggest lie of his life, in order to expiate the demons of his own past, in order to try and put things right, and win forgiveness from the woman he loved. At least Malcolm now would get a posthumous pardon, and his name would be cleared. That was the only thing he cared about; to somehow whiten the name of his best friend, when in his folly and youthful brashness he had blackened it. He didn't care about his own life; maybe now the ghosts of Malcolm and that sweet girl Roberta would rest in peace. As for himself, what did it matter when he knew he could never see his Jenny again? He was resigned now to his fate.

The soldiers beat him and buffeted him on the way back to the prison, where he would to wait an agonized three days before the sentence was carried out. All black and blue with bruising, both inward and outward, he arrived back in the same prison cell from which he had been taken. What did it matter, what did anything matter? He was about to die a gruesome death, for the sake of a point of honour; he could have saved his life, and told the truth, - that he had no idea what had become of the money. But he felt that blaming himself and letting the law take its fury out on him was the only honourable option. His death would be an expiation for his own miserable sin. Why had he not trusted and believed in Malcolm when he had the chance? Now all was lost - -

He sat, broken and bruised, in the jail once again, a different man than the one who had sat there this morning – a man who had now made his peace, with destiny, with the world, and with his past. Thoughts of Jenny once again rose unbidden, simply bursting with the glad light of the past into his consciousness. "Jenny his own and Jenny his love" no longer, but a Jenny who still illuminated his darkness.

CHAPTER 4

Within the Dungeon

"I KEN HOW YE feel laddie."
In the same dungeon, but not in the same cell - - Someone else was there.

Somerled had been sitting there with his face against the cold unyielding bars, hanging between a terrible void of lostness and a self-congratulating thought that he had done the right thing, that honour had been satisfied. Why then did wistful dreams of Malcolm and of Jenny interpose themselves, so that he had sobbed against the bars? Yes, that was just what he had been doing, he realised, without even being aware of it; the cold hard unyielding bars were wet with his own heart-rending tears. He should feel better about things now, now that his own atoning death was decided upon, lay ineluctably before him. Yet the image of Jenny he had dwelt on was not consoling, but only excruciating, - as if she were standing with her arms outstretched to him crying and pleading - -

"You don't know how I feel, you can have no idea how I feel." He said this almost bitterly, without looking round to see who had spoken to him.

"Ay ye think not, laddie, but I do. I know all the wiles of love, and everything it can drive a man to. Ye see, I'm am old man; that means I've experienced most things, and have as ye might say, a modicum of wisdom."

Somerled now turned to see who was speaking. There was indeed a very old-looking man against the opposite wall. He was rather wizened and white, very gaunt, yet with eyes which looked huge and seemed to shine with a light.

"Who are you?" asked Somerled. "How long have you been here?"

"Well ye see laddie, I'm a priest. Yes your eyes might widen but I'm what ye might call a popish priest, and I got lost and waylaid in this wild land of mountains and kirks and hatred toward the old ways. But that is what I am, for my sins be it said, a catholic espousing the Jacobite cause who has ended up incarcerated because on the wrong side. And I've been here in the darkness, a long while till I've lost the colour in my skin. Yet be that said, I still have a light in my soul to guide me. Aye, the lord God does not desert his own."

"But he has deserted me."

"Not so fast laddie, how do ye know the Lord has deserted you? Certainly don't lay it to his account because ye have ended up in a jail. Our Lord himself ye ken, has been imprisoned. And as it is written in Isaiah"- his eyes shone as he quoted the noble words of scripture - "I have given thee as a covenant to the people to bring out the captives from the dungeon."

"But your name, what is your name?"

"Why, laddie, why de ye need to ken my name? What is a name? I shall be the voice of God to you; the voice of God doesn't need a name attached. Indeed we mustn't speak God's name."

"My name is Somerled. And there shall ever be a terrible story attached to my name. I am someone who put his own head in the hangman's noose, and is due to die a traitor's death, in order to put right what I have done wrong in the past, and to earn forgiveness."

"Well, ye must ken laddie, forgiveness can't be earned; it is a free gift. Aye it is a free gift of God, and also between men it is a mercy that flows freely. Ye cannae put a price on it. "The quality of mercy is not strained, it droppeth as the gentle dew " - - Here he waxed lyrical as he quoted Shakespeare.

Somerled's brow contracted in consternation; here was a strange old man, sharing his cell, who remained peculiar and nameless, and was quoting the bible and Shakespeare at him! His interest in the old man increased as his eyes grew wide with a kind of wonder. Could he really be the voice of God to him, if he told him his story?

"Let me tell you my story," he said. And he began.

He told the whole story, in all the fine detail he could remember, without leaving anything out. His intoxicating first love for Jenny, his friend Malcolm's love for Roberta, how he had betrayed his friend by accusing him of stealing, who then ran away to France and got killed in battle, how he had spoken to Roberta who had ended her own life, how Jenny said she could never forgive him - -

"Aye laddie, but I've seen worse stories in confession. All men are sinners, prone to tragic mistakes, errors of judgement."

"But I betrayed my own best friend! And caused the deaths of two people Jenny loved – Malcolm, in whose house I met her, and her own best friend Roberta. And now to put it all right, to somehow atone for it, I took the blame myself, in order to exonerate Malcolm, to restore his name and honour. A traitor's death is no less than I deserve, because I have betrayed"- -

The old man was silent. It was a long silence, and Somerled looked toward him intently, wondering what verdict this old and wise man of God would pronounce on his action, - on the thing he had just done which instead of making him feel righteous again, only filled him with a sense of greater despair and loss.

"Listen to me laddie, and listen well." He paused. "I commend ye for trying to put things right, but in giving yourself up to death you have shown a misplaced sense of honour. Better to die for someone who is alive than, like you, to die for someone who is dead. Besides, she'll be waiting for you - - "

"Waiting for me - -?" The thought struck Somerled with almost physical force. "But she can't forgive me for her loss of - - "

"And what do ye think it will be like for her, to bear the loss of you too?" She has borne enough loss with the death of her two friends, without bearing the pain of your death too. She only said she would never forgive you because of her pain and sadness. She surely did not mean for you to go get yourself killed too in your despair. Death in despair is not the one of the ways of God, ye ken laddie. The way of God would be genuine forgiveness and reconciliation. Do ye really believe ye can restore things to rights by dying? No; God demands more of us than that. The noblest thing would be to seek her out. Wherever she is gone, to seek her out, open your heart to her, and let God in. Mark my words, she'll be waiting for you - -"

Somerled was dumb-struck. He turned his face away from the old man, and beat his head against the iron bars, which now really seemed like a cage, a cage of lost hope and idiocy, a cage of his own making. And he howled out of his raging sense of pain and loss and futility.

The nameless old man, who had made his pain worse, and yet had at the same time enlightened him, waited silently till the noise of his grief abated.

"Somerled," he whispered softly.

"What is it?" he replied, with a voice that sounded as though it came from a long way away, or from the grave.

"I know of a way out."

"A way out?! You mean a way out of despair, of endless lostness? You don't mean a way out of this dungeon do you?"

"I mean exactly that!"

A stunned silence came from Somerled. Yet from his heart there issued something like a wild, sweet, hope-filled song. It was full of the scent of heather, of magnificent mountains and tumbling waterfalls, issuing from somewhere very deep, as deep as the unfathomable judgements of God. "Jenny my own, Jenny my love, Jenny who with outstretched arms is waiting for me"!

<h1 style="text-align:center">CHAPTER 5</h1>

<h2 style="text-align:center">From the Fort</h2>

THERE WAS A prolonged silence in the prison cell, as Somerled adjusted to the new thing that now swam into his awareness. Up till now he had thought his doom was decided upon, the die cast, but a new perspective had opened up with the strange old man declaring there was a way out. Somerled's heart had bounded toward new bright hopes as the silence in the place remained palpable; you could have heard a pin drop.

"There is a way out- really?" Somerled's voice stretched between sounding incredulous and the excited wonder of a schoolboy who has just discovered the most delightful thing in the world.

"Leave your grip on those bars laddie, and come over here."

Somerled suddenly realised that all this while he had been gripping those cold unyielding bars, as if they were the only reality; they represented the constrained and narrow path of certain death to him. But now a new reality had presented itself. Deliberately and slowly he held the chain of his shackled wrists and shuffled across to the opposite corner of the cell. There he found the man who up until now had been only a disembodied voice.

He was far more frail than Somerled expected; just a thin remnant of a man, slumped against the wall as if he needed propping up. He was not dressed as a man of God, but merely in tattered rags. He looked as though he had been there through an aeon of slowly passing time. Indeed, Somerled wondered, how long had he been there, waiting to minister to a lost cause like himself?

The old man pointed. "Over there, over there," he stated with a kind of excitement in his voice.

Somerled went over to the far corner, to find a huge rock on the floor. It was a massive stone which had obviously been shuffled into place for a purpose.

"Underneath that rock there is a way out; there is a hole, and man could get through it. It leads down to the sewer system, which could lead you out beyond the fortification of the wall."

Somerled was on his knees examining the rock, feeling its crevices with his fingers in the semi-dark. "How do you know this old man?"

"I know because I've been here before."

On a rush Somerled became excited. He didn't pause to ask the old man how he had come to be in this dilemma on a previous occasion; he just put his shoulder to the stone to see if he could shift it. "yes I think I will be able to move it, given a little time."

"It's no good me trying to move it; I left that strength of youth behind me a long while ago. I could bewail the fact, but ye ken, but as Job says, "the lord giveth and the Lord taketh away" -

"Come over here," said the Somerled, "put your wrist-chains in that hollow, - yes so- that will help." He strained his best to move this huge rock which seemed to have become strangely symbolic to him. If he could shift this rock, then he could do anything; he could go and find Jenny, and he could find forgiveness. Yes the divine forgiveness which the old man had told him of, would be his if only he were man enough to shift this rock from the hole on which it rested.

Suddenly the memory came to him of his younger days with Malcolm and the sports they did together, and the tossing of the caber at which he so excelled. "This is for you" he whispered to the soul of his friend. And he gave a mighty heave, and there was a grating sound as the hole beneath the rock was exposed. "Our passage to freedom!" he simply stated.

There was a stink as the stale, foul air rose to meet them. He threw himself at the old man's feet; "Thankyou for this" he said eagerly, "I shall forever be in your debt." Then he added awkwardly, "you are coming with me, aren't you?"

"No laddie, I fear I shall not last long if I go with you. Something tells me it would not be wise."

"But you must come! Let me do something to thank you, by restoring you to your fortunes. Fortune must shine upon you if it shines upon me. I am indebted to you. I do not mean only for my escape but for the wisdom you gave me which made me desire to escape. I was locked in self-pity till you spoke to me. You have inspired me with a reason to live."

"Aye I may not have been a good priest, but I'm glad I spoke God's words to someone before the end of my days."

"It is time you told me your name" said Somerled, with affection and gently.

"My name doesn't matter laddie. Call me Father."

Somerled's eyes moistened; he was like the father he had never had, who had guided him by wise words, unlike his real father who never had the chance because of his untimely death. "Yes I will call you Father, and think of you as such for as long as my life lasts."

He tenderly picked up the old man and balanced him on his back, then both of them disappeared down the conduit.

Ten minutes later they were looking out of the other end of the conduit, where it emerged from the base of the prison. But it wasn't outside the fortification as Somerled had hoped, but rather inside. Somerled put his head back in, as he saw a soldier standing rather nonchalantly close by.

He carefully put down the old man. Of course he had no weapons; but he did have the chains round his wrist, which may serve in a fight. "Surprise was the best advantage" thought Somerled. He could see the soldier about to turn; it was now or never! He leapt forward with a clanking of the chain and secured it round his neck. The noose tightened, and the man fell.

There was sudden cry from the old man he had lain down. Turning he saw there was another soldier, one who had lurked unseen, who was now placing his bayonet against the old man's throat. Without having time to think, Somerled leapt upon him, and a struggle ensued, Somerled flailing with his manacled wrists whilst the soldier tried to get the better of him. In his gaunt thinness the old man stood, as if he would try to help. On the sudden the soldier's bayonet loosed from his grasp and seemed to speed straight into the old man's upper body. He fell back, and his head crashed with a sick thud against the wall. His skull seemed to shatter.

Somerled had got hold of the soldier's dagger and thrust it into his side, so he now collapsed in a heap. Then he approached with fear the sight of the good old man, slumped against a wall yet again, but this time with blood streaming from a head-wound. "All thanks to me" thought Somerled ruefully, so bitterly wishing that he had better protected his new-found friend, his spiritual father from who he had hoped to hear much wisdom and guidance on his future path. And now - -

He knelt beside him and cradled his head. "I spoke God's words to someone" faltered the man's voice, looking eerily far away. But his eyes were already glazed and unseeing. Somerled's heart broke and, despite the danger of the place, he sat and sobbed, the tears coursing down his cheeks.

The end when it came was imperceptible; a slightly longer sigh of a breath, and then he was still. The moment seemed eternal. Somerled's consciousness moved out into interstellar space where he seemed aware of the huge whirl of time and the vast moons knocking - -

"Fare thee well, old man – a Father to me." He kissed him gently on the forehead, and reverently laid his head on the ground. "I will never forget you."

Despite his crippling grief, which made him want to be immobile, he had to be gone. The soldiers he killed would soon be missed. He swallowed hard and deep, whisked the tears from his face, took a long gulp of air, surveyed the scene before him.

He took one last look at the man with a shattered skull, who forever after he would identify as his spiritual father, because in the last hours of life he had passed something onto him; his touch of wisdom. The old priest had prevented him from dying uselessly, had elucidated what forgiveness would truly look like, and told him that Jenny was in truth waiting for him. With that clear hope and faith, he now stood up and bounded the distance to his new freedom.

As he climbed the parapet, he heard the roar of a stag in the distance. The landscape seemed to open out to him, to welcome him in; there were wide horizons and unguessed possibilities. A short while ago what bounded his world was the cell of a dungeon and the certain finality of death; a death he chose to put things right. Now he had a mission to work out the divine purposes of forgiveness, whatever they might be. And there was the world before him, laid out at his feet. Where would he go? How could he seek Jenny? - -

As he made the dangerous leap into the safety and liberty of the woods, a great shout welled up from the depths of him – "Jenny his own, Jenny his love," Jenny who gifted him with freedom and hope!

CHAPTER 6

At the Bothy

THERE WAS NO hunt for him. The soldiers didn't chase him through the wood, as on the first occasion. Somerled didn't know why this should be; he presumed their attention was otherwise occupied by Jacobite matters. But he was grateful, even though the silence all around him was like a heavy weight upon his consciousness.

He pursued his way north-east through the glen of the Spean, amazed at his own gleefulness and sense of liberation. He had thought his life was ended in that prison cell, and suddenly, almost incomprehensibly, he now had life in front of him. It was all thanks to that good old man, who had given him all the wise counsel that he could, before finally dying in his arms. He stopped and panted for a bit, realising there was no need to keep on running. Straightening himself and stretching he looked to the south, and the magnificent Nevis Range struck him with its wild beauty. Now there was a mountain indeed!

He walked on at a brisk pace, frequently turning to gaze at the solid mountain heights, which even now in the summer was crowned with a wreath of snow. It made him think of that favourite mountain of his, where he used to walk as a teenager; those were his happy carefree days! But then he had met Jenny, and some sense of fate began to pursue him. Yet he was so happy in those early days with her; a bliss and rapture beyond most men's imaginings possessed his being, as though he had joined the life of the immortal gods. He was being fed with ambrosia, and food of angels, every time he talked with Jenny, until he seemed to grow into something different in nature than himself - - He rambled in his thoughts, as he pursued his way in silence through the landscape of mountains and glens.

Finally evening came, the sun was not far from setting, and he felt he had put enough distance between himself and the fort for one day. He sought for shelter and found a bothy attached to a sheep pen which would serve his purpose. Up till now he had only fled; tomorrow he must make more serious plans. There was a bit of food on one of the shelves; oats and kale. He devoured it voraciously. And there was a nearby stream from which he drank until his thirst was slaked. No sooner had he curled in the corner on the straw matting, than he was instantaneously asleep.

He slept the sleep of exhaustion for a while; the deep kind of sleep in which there are no dreams. But then a whole plethora of vivid dreams streamed through his brain, as though his mind were sorting through vast amounts of new material, trying to make sense in the light of what the old priest had told him of the whole pattern, the whole meaning - - It all seemed to stream into one image, the moment he had dreamed of so many times of Jenny's long black hair entangled in his hands, as he buried his head into her, and that waterfall containing the arch of a rainbow - -

He woke with a start, to see the early morning light streaming through the small aperture of the window. He was aware that the dream wasn't like it was in real life; in his memory of all the times he had held Jenny close to him, there was no waterfall and no rainbow. So what did that dream signify?

As he lay there, the morning slowly brightened and all the dawn chorus of bird-song flooded over his body mingled with the light; he lay in the foetal position very still. It was as if the very cool and white breath of God breathed over his body, telling him that he was loved. And he lay there for what seemed aeons, thinking, with pure clear thoughts falling into his still mind - -

He remembered all those sweet moments of holding Jenny's tresses, and the warm kisses he had showered on her, as if all those moments were threaded through and connected in the memory of

God. It was as if he saw the meaning of his life from God's point of view. This was the meaning of his life; loving and being loved.

He remembered the moment at the mill-house when Jennys' hand had lain on the cold stone, and he had taken it in his to fondle. And they simply stood there, the two of them, touching and stroking each others' hands. He was alive to the sensuousness of palms and finger-tips; it was unearthly. Suddenly she had reached up her hand to caress his cheek; it was a moment that was soft and sweet. But even softer and sweeter was the moment he bent and touched with his own lips those sensuous pouting lips of hers which were craning upwards. An explosion seemed to happen in his head, as for the first time he caressed her thick black hair, holding her close to him. That was the first time they had kissed.

There was another moment when they were crossing the burn by Malcolm's house. The rushing churning waters were in spate and it was not an easy stream to leap across as was usually the case. They had been climbing the forest of the mountain-side together, laughing and chattering to each other in all pleasantness. But then the rushing channel of bubbling water presented them with an obstacle. They weren't prepared to go the long way round when Malcolm's house was in sight. "I'll carry you" Somerled had declared on impulse. "No you can't - -" Jenny had squealed; "You will stumble and drown the two of us!" "Just you watch me!" he replied, catching her up, before manfully fording through the force of water.

They had collapsed laughing on the other bank. "Now look, you are all wet!" said Jenny. "And you are all dry!" he laughingly replied. Her pretty mouth and nose broke into a sweet dimpled smile while her deep brown eyes twinkled with mischievousness; "Oh Somerled MacKintosh, I do believe you are falling in love with me." "Too right I am!" he had cried in glee. And he had tumbled with her in the grass, pressing all of his body against hers, and burying his hands in that mass of hair, and showering kisses all over her face and neck - -

Yet another moment came to mind, when they were in the barn together, he helping her to care for the cow, and feed the chickens. "You know Jenny, I've been thinking, could we ever live a life together you and I?" She had suspended her throwing of the chicken-feed, and turned to smile at him. "I mean given," he continued, "that our families are on different sides of the battle which even now begins to rage- I hear the Prince has raised his standard at Glenfinnan, and I know that I must rally to his cause. Is it possible for us to be in love when this is happening around us, and your father " - - "Hush hush, Somerled!" She had come really close up to him and put her soft finger across his lips; "Don't speak of such things." She put her arms round his neck, and pouted those lips of hers again; a signal to him that she wanted to be caressed.

That was the day he had asked her to marry him. He had suddenly blurted it out, without considering carefully how they might get over the difficulties; her family on one side and he on the other in a war that was about to rage to put the true king on the throne. "Jenny I know you love me," he had said, "but can you marry me?" "She had fallen over his face with her hands and lips,- passing all over his face, kissing him. "Oh yes Somerled, yes, I want to be your wife."

Then in the sudden he remembered another moment; that was the barn, the same barn! About one year to the day from that sweet declaration of love to each other, he had found Roberta hanging from the rafters, swinging in front of him, dead. Now his thoughts suddenly turned ugly, and the sweetness of memories fled.

He remembered then how he had told Jenny, back in the house, what he had told Roberta about her beloved Malcolm. And there were streams of tears down Jenny's face, and she looked distraught with her hair all dishevelled, and she had cried heart-brokenly over the death of her friend, and she had blamed him. And she pronounced those words, "I shall never, not ever forgive you!"

Somerled suddenly opened his eyes, as with a moment of shock, from his reverie. "Malcolm was the lynchpin" he stated aloud in a voice of grief. Of the whole story, a tale of intense highs and lows, Malcolm had been the lynchpin. Everything turned on his betrayal of his friend. He would think about that some other time. "Betrayal, betrayal" - - seemed to echo round his head as he began to realise that the day had now turned into full morning, and it was time he was gone. He had made no plans of where to go, but go somewhere he must - -

He shook himself, as if to shake the sleep and memories from him. Handfuls of oats he shoved into his mouth, and stuffed into his pockets; they would provide energy for the road. As he opened the door and stepped into a sunlit meadow, his memories of those sunny times with Jenny once more struck into his mind. Yes, many golden days he had spent blissfully in Jenny's company, without suspecting the tragedy that was to come. "Jenny his own, Jenny his love, Jenny of the pouting lips and thick black hair, who once wanted to marry him" - -

CHAPTER 7

Among the Mountains

THAT MORNING, WITH all the bright sunlight and birdsong around him, he decided on a course of action. He would pursue his way northward toward the wild and desolate area of the Moidart region.

His intense day-dreaming about Jenny seemed to have cleared his head and produced some kind of plan. He knew she had family in the North, in a village called Durness; they may know where she had gone. That summer, that glorious romantic summer they had together, had happened because she was visiting her aunt's family, Malcolm being her half-cousin.

As he pursued his way through the large mountainous and unforgiving landscape his mind automatically turned again to that summer with Jenny, the summer which never seemed to end in its goldenness, its playful happiness. The four of them – the two friends Jenny and Roberta, and himself and Malcolm – thought that golden time was eternal in quality and would never end. If they had fleetingly considered its ending they saw it in terms of a riot of marriages, for Malcolm was in love with Roberta as Somerled was with Jenny. It was just idyllic, even it was though presaged by another rebellion for the true king in their homeland. But battles seem a long way away when lovers are wooing.

He trudged many miles, until He finally reached Glencarron, and saw the beauty of the sea-loch below him as he stood on the cliffs. It was here, with a sparkling view, that his mind was jolted by the words he had announced on waking from his reverie in the bothy, - "Malcolm was the lynchpin." It turned his mind onto a completely different thought-path.

He now started to think about his boyhood friend, overwhelmed by a sickening sense that he had betrayed him. He remembered the time when they had been playing with fake soldier's swords on the knoll by his mother's cottage, and as his mother called them in to eat, they had embraced and sworn an eternity of friendship. "We shall always be friends, always." - - And now his friend was disgraced and dead due to his own stupid actions.

He remembered the time in the barn, - that same terrible barn in which so many dire events of his young life were enacted – when they swore to be blood-brothers, cutting themselves so as to commingle their blood. And he had betrayed his own best friend! – the friend who was no less important than Jenny, and whose friendship had lasted far longer, right back into the mists of early childhood. How could he have betrayed him? – by a single act in a single moment of time, annulling all the gracious gift of the twenty years that had gone before?

He thought about it; he thought about it intensely as he strode onwards, continually northwards. So if Malcolm were indeed the lynchpin, as his deeper dreaming mind seemed to be telling him, Malcolm had to be the centre of his mistakes – Malcolm and not Jenny, though it was Jenny's cry of perpetual unforgivingness and his loss of her which was making his heart ache the more. Maybe if he concentrated on Malcolm's part in this, the maze of his memories would fall into place and make sense. - -

He walked many days into what seemed a wilderness, with strange-shaped mountains standing erect out of a wild uninhabited country, and looming out of the mist. He pondered at length over his betrayal of his Malcolm; as he thought about it the more, the more he felt deeply ashamed. It hadn't happened at all as he had reported in the tribunal at the fort. He hadn't stolen the money himself and falsely implicated Malcolm. What happened was far more complicated than that.

Somerled was initially chagrined to find Malcolm wanted to fight on the opposite side of the conflict, due to the complexity of clan loyalties, whilst Somerled's sympathies were fiercely for the Jacobite cause. They had argued it out, and Somerled finally agreed to switch sides in order to assist Malcolm with his difficult commission of accompanying the gold which was meant to resupply the garrison of soldiers at Fort William. The war had cruelly divided clan against clan, friend against friend, and Somerled wanted to perform this one act of camaraderie, for pure friendship's sake.

There had indeed been a waterfall and a glen that night, when they were conscious of the danger of carrying a large amount of gold coin north. He had heard noises in the night and got up to see Malcolm stuffing pebbles into one of the panniers. "Where's the gold gone?" Somerled had queried in surprise. "Shh" Malcolm had insisted, "it's hidden under that rock by the waterfall." "What are you doing?" Somerled had shouted, alarmed and surprised, thus rousing the other men. And then the cry went up and they had fallen upon Malcolm without further querying. As he was bound he hissed at Somerled between his teeth- "Somerled, it was for a purpose!"

But Somerled never found out what that purpose was. Malcolm had been incarcerated, and Somerled was not allowed to see him; not until that moment when he was called to speak and give witness in court against his own best friend - - He hadn't at the time thought there could be "a purpose"; he feared Malcolm was guilty. And the pain and torment of it all, torn between his sense of honour in telling the truth and his honourable duty to stand by his best friend, drove him beserk. Also attention was focused upon him when he was apparently acting on the wrong side of the conflict, which caused no end of complexity and guilt. It was almost a sense of relief when Malcolm was condemned as a traitor - -

But now Somerled could see there may have been "a purpose," a good reason for what Malcolm was doing. Maybe he knew of a genuine robbery that was going to happen on the road ahead and he was trying to protect and hide the gold; there were all sorts of possible scenarios. But the point is, he should have stood by his friend, he should have believed in him! Somerled could see that now;

he should have stood by the friend he loved, not just testified against him. What he did amounted to a betrayal of his best and lifelong friend.

Somerled had gone a long way by now, on the day he reached this conclusion. He lay down beside a stone ruin halfway up a mountain side and closed his eyes. But the terrible thoughts and dreams did not leave him alone; they were like harpies round his head. As his eyes closed he remembered Jenny's voice screaming at him – "But you betrayed your friend! And I love Malcolm!"

Hold on; she said she loved Malcolm! When He had first heard this, he thought she meant that she merely loved Malcolm as a friend, as Somerled's friend, and as her own distant cousin. But supposing she meant something else? Could he have been mistaken all along, and that it was Malcolm she loved rather than himself? A great gaping chasm yawned at his feet, and he seemed to fall into it. - -

The next thing he knew he was asleep in a kind of fitful nightmarish dream; the tortured faces of Malcolm, Jenny and Roberta all revolved around, accusing him. Then it paused and the scene opened on the kitchen of Malcolm's house, which had been the focus of such happy times. There had been a small keepsake he had given to Jenny in those happy times, - a brooch – and now in the dream, Malcolm deliberately laid it in front of him on the table - -

He woke with a shock; that had truly happened! How did it come to be in Malcolm's possession? Had Jenny thought so little of it as to give it to him? He had thought nothing of it at the time, but now it all made sense - - Malcolm was claiming Jenny as his own! It all made sense now; that was why she was so furiously angry about what had happened, and why she was so completely broken-hearted - -

He stood up; he had been so deeply drawn into his thought-life that he had been oblivious as to where he was. He saw that he was on the high slope of a rugged mountain, and the sunset was just breaking into multi-coloured layers of light above him, with the orange rays of the sinking sun striking horizontally the ground around him. The air was very chill.

This was the end for him; it had suddenly apparently realised that Jenny was in love with Malcolm, and not himself! His heart seemed to break in two as he stood there on the mountain-side, surrounded by the lovely light, alone.

He looked down to the left and saw a croft beneath him, with a lazy smoke winding from its chimney; hopefully he could find the warmth of a hearth there. But how could he ever find warmth anywhere if what he saw were indeed the truth? He had walked far enough into the wilderness, and had contemplated the truth; it was time for his return. But oh Jenny, whom he had thought "Jenny his own, Jenny his love,"- how could ever live without her?!

CHAPTER 8

Toward the North

SOMERLED CAME DOWN the lonely mountainside like a man who was unseeing, like a man on whom the sorrow of the world weighed visibly. Only one thought filled his whole consciousness - maybe his beloved Jenny had loved Malcolm and not himself - - - Every leaden step betrayed his burdened agony at this thought.

He found the croft, where he had hoped he could find the warmth of a hearth for the night. They gave him food and were kind to him; they could see some great affliction weighed upon him, but said nothing. This only made Somerled's loneliness more acute, as he set off again the next morning. He had been aiming with a narrow purpose for Jenny's home village, to get news of her. Now the road before him seemed wide and spacious, and it seemed only the damned walked there - -

He came across a deep ravine, into which water plunged relentlessly, making a din in his ears. He sat on the edge and felt the despair of a man who is close to being tempted to take his life. He looked down into the chasm below, suspended between varying impulses - -

Suddenly the voice of the man he had called "Father," the old man who had rescued him from the death which faced him in the prison, rang in his ears; "Death in despair is not one of the ways of God, ye ken laddie; the way of God would be genuine forgiveness and reconciliation. Do ye really believe ye can restore things to rights by dying? God demands more of us than that."

Somerled drew back suddenly from the edge; No, he would think no more of that! He must try and be worthy of that old man gifting him with life, setting him free; he must try and be worthy of that old man's sacrifice of his own life to get him away from that stinking prison, out into the freedom of fresh air.

What should he do now, - wander broken and purposeless for the rest of his life, or take the old man's counsel? What else had he said? – "The noblest thing would be to seek her out; wherever she is gone, to seek her out, open your heart to her, and let God in. Mark my words, she'll be waiting for you."

Somerled wasn't so sure any more about the latter, if she never really loved him, but he would follow the old man's counsel, and seek her out. Yes, that's what he would do, he vowed, as he stood up with resolution. "My Father" he whispered to himself, "I shall take the wise advice of my Father." And so he went on his way, heading North.

A few days later he came upon the most northern seaboard of mainland Scotland, and to a scarcely populated village called Durness. This is where he knew Jenny had family. Somerled felt very tired by now. His time in the lonely mountainous region had hollowed him out. In his past he would have said that he was hollowed out to the purpose of being more filled, - aye in his past! Now he felt that he had been hollowed out forever. He felt empty and spent.

He found out by asking directions that Jenny's father lived at the end of the village, in what was by far the most large and well-apportioned house, though all of them were small. He approached it hesitantly. He had been walking hundreds of miles over a wild stretch of mountainous terrain, catching food and shelter where he could, and must appear dirty, smelly and unkempt. He put a hand to his long beard and hair, and his courage began to fail him. But then another evening was fast approaching - -

He knocked solemnly on the door. The thud- thud seemed to fall on deaf ears, because no-one answered him. "Is anybody there?" he called, feeling himself a lonely mendicant traveller, who would only get rejected.

Jenny had spoke well and warmly of her father, as a man of honour and compassion; he had to believe in that now, as he had come all this way to plead with him. This man would have been his Father, if he had married Jenny as he'd planned; a man to replace his dead father whom he had hardly known. At the moment because the old man before his untimely death at the fort had said "call me Father," Somerled could honestly say he believed in Fathers. He would trust to that now, and he knocked again.

With still no reply, it occurred to him to be less formal and to look round the back of the house. His idea was rewarded for there was the mother of the house, hanging out the washing. As she turned her care-worn face toward him, Somerled instantly knew it was Jenny's mother. For the contours of the face were so similar to hers; the same finely chiselled features, and great dark eyes, and thick hair which was now tied back and greying. He was stunned for a minute, then felt he must reply, for she was asking "Yes, can I help you?"

"I've been knocking. May I speak with Jenny's father?" he said, as clearly as he could in the face of his emotion.

"Yes of course; he's in the back kitchen, doing the accounts. As he'd told me he wanted peace, he no doubt thought that I would answer the door."

She went in, and a short moment later her husband came out, looking in a querying manner at Somerled. "So you are the young man?"

"No I'm not the young man," said Somerled with a strong memory of that moment on the mountain when he thought he saw clearly that "the young man" in question was Malcolm and not himself - - "that is, I'm not certain whether I am the young man or not."

"Mm, this is a pretty kettle of fish, and no mistake."

The man seemed rather distressed, and didn't seem inclined to invite him in, or not even to take his hand, as Somerled courteously extended his.

A certain distress suddenly grasped Somerled. He had come so very far, he had trusted that he would receive some kindly form of help from Jenny's parents; in fact he hadn't considered otherwise. So this coldness broke him down. He collapsed on his knees and let out a sob.

Maternal hands were instantly about him; "Didna fret yeself, noo, didna fret!"

Maybe this was the one approach he could have best made to Jenny's parents,- that of the stranger in distress and need. For they were a kind-hearted couple who had an open and generous heart toward those on whom fortune declines to smile. They had experienced much good fortune themselves – abundant harvests, the flourishing of two golden children into adulthood; one comely and gracious, the other gone off to fight against the Jacobites, and yet returned home unscathed. A good providence smiled on them, and influenced by genuine Christian sympathies, they tried to alleviate the lot of those who suffer.

"What is it lad?" said the man, as the mother smothered him with caresses. The father came forward "Are you not the Somerled of whom she spoke?"

Somerled's heart bounded in his chest at the words - - "the Somerled of whom she spoke"? Not Malcolm then? "Yes, Yes" he replied, half with a happy grin and half with a sob, "Yes I am Somerled."

"We've been instructed by her not to tell anyone where she has gone," the Father said in a tone of sadness, "and especially not you. What happened between ye two, what terrible thing happened to make her say that? But come in laddie, come in and rest yeself awhile."

To hear that term of affection used again- "laddie" – as the old man had used it in that festering prison-cell, recalling him from his dire purpose to a better path – made Somerled's heart crack with a sense of pity. It was pity for himself, and pity for Jenny, and pity for those two who had died due to his malign influence on their lives, those two lovely lovers Malcolm and Roberta. So he limped into the house, leaning on the arm of Jenny's mother, collapsed and wretched, but with a vague sense of hope.

And as he waited in the kitchen of Jenny's mother, the kitchen in which she herself must have so happily grown up, whilst this kindly lady went to fetch the warm griddle-cakes, with the butter and fruit-jam, and the reviving ale she had promised, - as all this wonderful food was tantalizingly about to appear, he leaned back in the coolness, silence and solitude. He felt he had found a refuge at last, after all his wanderings, a place dear to Jenny's own heart where he could rest. "Jenny his own, Jenny his love," whose tender heart and caring hands were even now about him!

CHAPTER 9

At the Harbour

SOMERLED OPENED HIS eyes to peruse the cool morning light as it slanted in from the window. The bed he lay in had been Jenny's bed and the room Jenny's room. He felt refreshed and relaxed after a good nights sleep, after a good wash and good meal had helped to revive his sense of being human the night before. Yes, he felt human again, less like a wild thing come in from the wilderness; he felt akin to this kindly couple and belonging to this more civilised existence, hallowed by memories and contiguity with the love of his heart. He lay back in the delicious surroundings as he slowly revived to full consciousness.

There was a knock on the door. "Aye, I'm awake" he called out.

He suddenly recalled how the night before he had pressed Jenny's parents- Jock and Jean McIver - to reveal to him her whereabouts, but they had steadfastly refused to reveal it, saying they had made a solemn promise to their daughter. Maybe today he could change their minds.

"There's breakfast ready in the kitchen" piped up Jean McIver, "when ye are ready for it." There was silence again when she had bustled away from the door.

The pure magic and white light of the room had been disturbed now. He knew lying in bliss was not something he could easily do this side of the grave. He might as well get up, and face the reality of whatever the day had in store for him. Where would he be spending the next night, he wondered.

Jock and Jean McIver gave him a sumptuous breakfast. He had had a good rest in this place which had seemed a haven; were they now going to refuse to help him further?

Sitting back and reaching for his pipe in this kitchen which had so enchanted the visitor last night, the father of the family now seemed inclined to discuss things in depth and with greater frankness. Gone their daughter was, and she had fled from the pursuit of this man, though heaven knows, she must have loved him once. Whatever had passed between them, he felt sorry for the suffering of their youth, and was inclined to give a father's helping hand if possible.

"What made ye fight for the Jacobite cause? It broke Jenny's heart that ye espoused the opposite side."

His opening gambit had been wide and aggressive. But with a father's solicitude he was fishing, to find out what exactly had broken Jenny's heart, for she had never told them. She had only come back wide-eyed and distraught, her grief locked in silence, and said that her lover might pursue her, so she was going away again.

Somerled was taken aback by the question. He had every right to espouse which cause he chose, and it was certainly not this issue which broke Jenny's heart. He spoke with accentuated respect; "Sir, when the true Prince raised his standard at Glenfinnan I with many other clansmen felt it was right to restore the royal line. The domination of the English had to come to an end They do not know us, or understand our ways. Sir, I respectfully suggest, this had no bearing on the breaking of your daughter's heart."

"Aye, what was the cause of it then? She spoke of Malcolm and Roberta and she spoke of you, and she seemed happy. Then all of a sudden all was weeping, and she came here, grabbed belongings, and left us. As for the young Pretender, he had a whipping and no doubt; I hear he is still limping through the country, begging support and sympathy from any who will give it."

"No, not the pretender, but the true King! He is seeking the throne which is rightfully his! And if the clansmen are still giving him aid in the western isles it's because thy love him and know where their allegiance should lie!"

Somerled had flashed red with anger over the subject, but suddenly he calmed and said with the regret of genuine sadness; "I'm sorry if I helped to break the heart of your daughter. Believe me, I didn't mean to do it."

"But what happened, man? Are ye not going to tell us what happened!"

Joan McIver at this point, hearing her husband's raised voice whilst washing the dishes, turned to them and Somerled saw there were tears standing in her eyes. "You men, all ye can talk about is battles and wars and kings, when I have a daughter I have lost due to circumstances I cannot understand! Husband ! - - "

As Joan appealed to her husband and they both turned to look at Somerled, he blushed red to roots of his hair at the painful thought of how he had hurt Jenny. He silently got up from his chair, excused himself, and walked out into the air.

Outside in the garden all the birds were singing, and Somerled turned to peruse the house of Jenny's childhood. He could hear Jean McIver remonstrating with her husband in the kitchen.

Then there was silence for a minute, and it was clear Jenny's father was being influenced by the womanly sympathies of the mother. For he came out, put an arm round Somerled and said, "Aye laddie, I'll take you out in the boat, and we'll go fishing."

An hour later the two men sat in the middle of a calm bay called Skerray harbour. The shore made a great curve at this point, nearly meeting itself on the other side, so they the blue sea lapped quietly on the shores of a little cove, reflected the blue sky. All the pebbles of the beach made a gentle rattling sound as the waves gently stirred and rubbed them against each other. It was a beguilingly magical place, a secret place of beauty and calm.

"Jenny wrote of you as the love of her heart" stated Jock, in a calm and ponderous voice. He was obviously not a man of many words, and always expressed himself concisely.

"She wrote of me - - " stammered Somerled, "not Malcolm?" Somerled was only too glad to hear this, having developed the fixated idea that Jenny must have loved Malcolm.

"Why Malcolm?" Jock said with a surprised voice, "She loved Malcolm as her cousin of course, and we still get news of him where he is in France."

Somerled nearly fell out of the boat with shock. "Malcolm- alive! But I caused his death, I betrayed him - -"

Jock calmly saw to the fish he had just caught and showed no great reaction to Somerled's extreme emotion. Somerled got hold of the both sides of the boat in an effort to calm himself, and breathed deeply as he tried to process this massive chunk of new information.

Why, this changed everything! If Jenny didn't love Malcolm and Malcolm were still alive - - A sudden rosy glow sprung up somewhere in the middle of Somerled, a place where there had only reigned despair - - And of course, if this were true, maybe Jenny could forgive him - - But then why had she run away from him? Why had she forbidden her parents to tell him where she was going?

"Is Jenny alright? Is she well?" Suddenly his solicitude was for her, rather than for his own sorry state.

"What can you say to me to convince me that ye love her, and will marry her?" said Jock, as his hands plied the fisherman's craft.

"Upon my honour Sir!" declared Somerled with a warm gush, "I do love her forever and always. She is like the air which I breathe which I cannot live without; she is like the earth on which I walk and bright canopy of the stars above. She is necessity to my very life; she is my very life, the best essence of my self. Her long thick hair and deep dark eyes and those pouting lips are a very part of the essence of my soul; she is my bright star, my angel! And upon my honour sir, if I can find her and persuade her to forgive me, I will love and cherish her all my days, and give her the best of myself, and make sure she wants for nothing and is always happy!"

There was silence, as the boat rocked to and fro gently on the waves, and the swishing of the pebbles continued on the strand, and sea and sky met in an embrace of blueness.

"I believe you," said Jenny's father, his voice sounding loud in that silence. "And as her Father who has a care for her greater welfare, I will tell you where she is gone."

And as he was told that Jenny had departed to work in one of the big houses in the plotted and pieced farmland of Fife, Somerled's soul seemed to crack out of his body and soar into the blueness around him as he perceived the possible truth of the words "she'll be waiting for you." - - Jenny his own, Jenny his love, whom he dared in this moment to hope would one day be his!

CHAPTER 10

Inside the Garden

SOMERLED WAS RIDING his swift brown horse through the mountain glens down the Eastern side of the country toward the kingdom of Fife. The horse's name was Piebald and Jock McIver, having a kindly heart for Somerled at the last, especially after his protestations of love for his daughter Jenny and his promise to look after her, had loaned him this magnificent and sturdy mare. Piebald was magnificent to Somerled because after a week of trudging through the Scottish wildlands on foot, this seemed a splendid, easy and speedy way to travel. It gave him speed straight to Jenny's heart, for he was convinced, now he knew that Malcolm wasn't dead, that as the old man in the prison had said, his Jenny would be "waiting for him."

Hundreds of miles he travelled, swift and straight as an arrow, over mountains and through glens, by the side of lochs and through forests, eager just to get to Jenny, to say he was sorry, to throw himself at her feet, to say that he loved her, that though he made a tragic mistake and tragic consequences followed, yet she could be sure of his devoted heart. Occasionally he glimpsed the sea, a grey and slowly heaving mass of water on his left, but always he rode on, buoyed up by hope and expectation.

Finally he cantered into Fife. He gazed around him at the gently rolling hills, and arable land plotted and pieced, like the coverlet for a gigantic bed which stretched all around him. It was fertile land indeed; he could smell the fertility in the air, the deep rich scent of crops and animals and manure. It was different from his own country and the crofting system with its meagre pickings. This was like a feast of fecundity. It pleased him; it made him feel gay, and full of hope. Surely nothing bad could happen in such a place, so luxuriantly filled with nature's blessings.

He enquired of the castle Jenny's father had named. Before he headed that way he stayed at one of the inns in a small Fife village. He ate and drank, being very hungry, and thirsty enough to drink a bottomless cup. He slammed the tankard down on the bench with a great satisfaction. Tomorrow he would be seeing Jenny. He didn't know her circumstances; her father hadn't explained much about it, but he was full of rosy hopes as he went to bed.

But he didn't sleep well at first; he tossed and turned with a sort of anxiety. Then when he did fall asleep that constant dream which had so often haunted him came back with force,- his head and hands deep in Jenny's thick black tresses and the resounding waterfall with the rainbow arched in its mist, and some strange cry - - He woke in a cold sweat; what did that dream signify? But then he relaxed after that, and enjoyed a deep refreshing sleep; he was so very tired.

The next morning he saddled his horse, payed with the scant coinage also loaned to him from Jock McIver, - his prospective father in law had been so very kind to him- and set off cool and confident to find his Jenny, - as cool and confident as could be expected, given that he was on fire with a rosy and passionate sense of romantic love.

An hour later Somerled was lashing Piebald's lead till it was firmly fixed by the entrance to the castle in question. He looked up at the many turrets and narrow windows, and felt rather intimidated. Knocking at the grand doors of castles was not something he generally did, but courage! his Jenny was in their somewhere, his own Jenny who had once said she wanted to be his wife.

A servant answered, and told him Jenny was working in the kitchen, if he could come round the back through the garden. His own Jenny working apparently as a kitchen maid; what would have induced her to do that? But Somerled obediently entered the walled garden which was indicated.

The beauty of the garden took Somerled's breath away. There was a profusion of roses, hollyhocks, and lavender, and lazy bees were buzzing in the heart of every flower. The sense of profusion overwhelmed him, the sense of some magical secret place where finally he would be led to Jenny.

Before he reached the door, it opened of its own accord, and there his Jenny stood, in the midst of all the flowers, moving toward him. Somerled felt himself running toward her, for his heart bounded with pleasure. Did they run toward each other or was that Somerled's imagination? For suddenly there she stood, in a neat blue frock and white apron, with her hand held out to stop his impetuous rush forward.

"What are you doing here?" she asked, coldly.

"Jenny my own - - " stammered Somerled, checked by her coldness.

Jenny now stood before him with folded arms. "I told my parents to tell no-one where I was gone." Her tone was unforgiving and imperious.

"But Jenny - -" Then Somerled decided not to appeal by simply telling of his undying love for her. It was his mistake. A woman can be turned by an impassioned plea of love, when a rational explanation will fall on deaf ears.

Instead what the old man had said in the dank prison cell echoed in his ears: "the way of God would be genuine forgiveness and reconciliation - - wherever she is gone, seek her out, open your heart to her, and let God in."

He pleaded with her to understand. "Jenny, I was willing to give my life to restore Malcolm's blackened name. I said it was myself who stole the money, I was condemned to death in the fort, and nearly died - - Yes if it weren't for that good old man - - He told me Jenny that I needed to seek you out and obtain your forgiveness."

"My forgiveness?" echoed Jenny in a puzzled voice.

"Yes, your father told me Malcolm is not dead after all, but keeps somewhere in France, and I thought - - "

"You thought what?" demanded Jenny, sounding cross.

"Well I thought that it would help you to forgive me, if I hadn't caused his death."

Jenny turned on him with an explosion of cold wrath. "And what about Roberta? Have you forgotten the image of her dead body hanging before your eyes? And her cold dead body laid out between the two of us? And how I told you then that Roberta was my best friend, dearer to me than even you were – Yes Somerled, dearer to me than you – And how I watched her heart break and bleed when you told her that her beloved Malcolm, whom she was due to marry Somerled, yes, marry! – how I watched her break down in utter grief when you so nobly and thoughtlessly told her that her Malcolm had done something so dishonourable as to steal the gold! Yes you so nobly and thoughtlessly broke her heart beyond what she could endure, telling her that you so nobly had to testify against your own best friend, condemning him to death!"

Taken aback by her bitter outburst, Somerled hung his head. "It doesn't seem that I acted very nobly does it?"

"Faithfulness to friends comes above all, Somerled, above all! And you betrayed your own best friend, and so tortured my best friend as to make her take her own life! How can I forgive you, Somerled, how can I forgive you?! You are not the man I thought you were!"

She turned on her heels and stalked out of the garden, disappearing into the door out of which she came.

Tears stung in Somerled's eyes. The garden was suddenly quiet and empty; he didn't see the flowers any more; he didn't see anything except his own shame and undoing. Slowly and lost in the throws of an infinite pain he made his way back to his horse. Slowly he rode away on Piebald like a man going to his doom.

There was nothing in front of him now. He realised he felt now what Roberta had felt when her marriage and her future had been snatched away from her! He never knew till now what pain he must have caused Roberta, or Jenny either, still mourning and bitter over the loss of her closest friend.

The landscape didn't look the same now as when he had ridden in high hopes this morning. He thought he could so easily get Jenny to forgive him, considering that Malcolm was not dead - - how wrong he was! He thought forgiveness could come cheap and easy; just an explanation, and the saying of sorry - -But Jenny's embattled heart was proof against him. And those dreadful words – "You are not the man I thought you were!" He let out a sob, as those words came home. "Jenny his own, Jenny his love," who now filled him with a sense of infinite loss.

CHAPTER 11

Upon the Sea

SOMERLED WAS WALKING amongst the lobster pots which were strewn along the pier in the Fife fishing village of Crail. He felt caught and trapped. He had come so far, seeking Jenny and her forgiveness, feeling that once he found her, it would be easy. And now having finally reached her, she had coldly spurned and rejected him. What was he to do now? There was nowhere to go; it was a dead-end.

A fisherman hailed him, waving and greeting him, from where he stood sturdily in his boat. Somerled was buried in his own sorrow, and hardly responded. The whole world seemed dead to him; why should he care about a Fife fisherman in his boat? He moved over to the outer arm of the little harbour and watched the great grey mass of the sea heaving and splashing against the grey stone. It was like a metaphor of life in some way; life just beat upon you until it wore you away. Where were his hopes and dreams now? All buried in those terrible words of Jenny's – "You are not the man I thought you were." Maybe out there in the middle of the vast sea things would make sense - - for some reason he grasped at this, and he went back to the kindly fisherman and asked "Can I come out in your boat with you?"

Half an hour later Somerled was bobbing up and down on the wide sea, the fisherman having responded by taking him aboard. He said he was not intending to fish but to collect lobster pots, but having led a solitary life, he quite welcomed the idea of company. The young man looked quite downcast he thought, obvious a wealthy young man who had been a fighter in the recent battles and fallen on hard times. Somerled's appearance had by now a certain shabbiness, a worn look as if the world had treated him badly. The older and wiser seaman felt sorrow over Somerled's apparent bruising in the affairs of the heart. He could see that whatever ailed Somerled it was a wound that was sufficient to break him, and he was in need of solace. A trip upon the ocean could provide solace; he knew that, and perhaps the younger man knew it too.

They rode in silence upon the grey waves for some while, the wind whipping against their faces and feeling cold; the mood of the day seemed to presage rain. Then all of a sudden a different wind sprang up and drove back the grey clouds, and the sun broke out and surged free, reflecting and dancing from the blue water. Somerled was astonished at the sudden change; all had been threatening and grey, and the next moment all was blue and scintillating with light.

He turned to the fisherman, suddenly seeing him clearly for the first time. "Sorry, I was lost in myself, this is beautiful. Are there often such changes on the sea? My name is Somerled, and much the worse for wear I'm afraid. What is your name, and how long have you worked at this trade? Is it your own boat?"

The older man smiled with pleasure, in that he could see Somerled had been led out of himself by the sudden beauty of the moment. He took a long slow pleasure in his answer. "My name is Willy; I've plied these seas, - the mackerel and the lobsters you know – for well-nigh forty years, - man and boy, aye man and boy! I learnt the craft for my father and he from his father. Our family have always farmed the sea, and it yields us a good and profitable harvest. And aye it's the family boat, rowed many a season- fair and foul weather, aye fair and foul. As for your other question –aye, it's like this out here on the sea, - we see sudden turns of light, - aye just like the landlubbers life, we get sudden turns of fortune."

Somerled reflected in silence for a bit, whilst the oars plashed in the blue sea and the boat made steady headway in the idyllic conditions. "Sudden turns of fortune" – yes he had experienced those. He suddenly wondered whether this older fisherman with the weather-beaten face and gnarled hands could provide him with more wisdom, like the old man had in the dank prison-cell. "I wonder if you can help me?" he said, voicing his thoughts aloud.

"Well I'll try, I'll certainly try; if you tell me what ails you."

Somerled's whole sorry story fell out of him, as if it had been held back by a bulwark until that moment. He ended by telling how Jenny had rejected his overtures in the garden, in a voice that sounded like a sob.

There was silence; the fisherman said nothing as he pulled in the lobster pots. "I'm trapped like one of these lobsters, aren't I?" said Somerled in a voice breaking with emotion.

"Half the wisdom of life," replied Willy slowly, "is in rightly seeing the situation. Now you are still alive, and Jenny is still alive - you must give thanks for that - and your friend is still alive. You must examine your options, aye your options." The man was obviously straining himself in trying to give a wise answer to the younger man; he wasn't used to the role as he was a fisherman with scant education.

He thought some more, with Somerled hanging on every word. "Either you abandon the love of your life, your Jenny, telling yourself it is not worth pursuing - and you will probably live on like a shade, trying to console yourself as best you may. Or else you do not let go of it - you say to your soul Jenny is truly your own and your love. You do what the man you called your Father in the prison told you – "seek her out, open your heart to her, and let God in." You didn't really open your heart to her, now did you?"

That was enough; that was all he needed to say. For Somerled now sat there silently gazing at the blue ocean around him, mulling over in his mind every word that was said in the garden. And he saw where he had gone wrong; instead of declaring his love for her he had tried to explain and justify himself. He saw clearly the reality of Jenny's abiding pain and how he had not addressed it, not found a way of opening their hearts to each other. He had failed to plead for a forgiveness that he didn't deserve and which lay alone in Jenny's gift - -

Nothing more was said between the two men in the boat. They both knew enough had been said, and gazing on the wide expanse of the ocean was all Somerled now needed to do to correctly see the situation, to make his choice of the options presented, to see what to do. He arrived back at the pier a chastened and a different man.

As he stepped out of the boat he turned and grasped the man's hand, holding his fingers firmly round the wrist for a moment and clenching in friendship. "How can I ever thank you?"

"No need to thank me," Willy the fisherman humbly said, "the good Lord works his wonders on the deep."

"He does indeed!" said the younger man with a lightness of heart, glad to be back on firm land. He knew now what choice he made; he could not cease to have his Jenny in his soul without destroying the meaning of his own life, and reducing himself to a shadow. He had to find a way of sorting this, he had to go back, and have a better, deeper talk with her; some kind of confession, which would reach right into the heart of that divine forgiveness which alone could reconcile them.

Two hours later, having refreshed himself first, and thought about what he could or should say, he was back at the same castle, having lashed his horse outside, and knocking fervently at the kitchen door. When it opened he spoke like a snowball of energy: "I must speak with Jenny!"

"She's gone!"

"Gone?!" And Somerled's heart and hopes broke inwardly. He almost collapsed, and had to steady himself by grasping the doorpost.

"If you are Somerled, there is a letter for you."

A minute later the letter was thrust into his hands. As he foreknew, it was from Jenny and written in her hand. He opened and read it feverishly, standing there in the garden which was woven with the colourful flowers of the season.

"Don't pursue me Somerled," it said; "I don't want to see you or speak with you again. I did sincerely love you once, but you have broken my heart. Nothing can ever be the same again. How could you be so thoughtless? You believed in acting nobly; how could you so throw lives away by your thoughtless deeds and words? You have destroyed lives around me Somerled, and screwed up my own heart. How could I ever forgive you? I am not your Jenny anymore, so don't call me that. You must leave me to go free - - Jenny."

Somerled with an automatic reaction crumpled it in his hands, and threw it among the flowers. And on his knees in that empty flower-filled garden silent tears coursed down his cheeks.

Half an hour later, after what seemed like an eternity of pain, he stood up, picked up the crumpled piece of paper, and spoke a vow, with a strength of soul he never knew he had. "I am truly sorry for what I have done, and I see what hurt I have caused. "Jenny my own, Jenny my love," I shall not stop calling you that, for I swear before the Christ who forgave us on the cross, I shall never stop seeking you, until I can speak deeply enough to you to bring forgiveness flowing between us - -

He rode on for hours, not knowing were he was going, blind and unseeing with his outward eyes, whilst the reality of another's pain came vividly and luridly to light inwardly. Yes he saw, now, he saw it all! He thought she was "Jenny his own, Jenny his love," but now he saw he had done something so ignoble that he could never hope to earn her or to win her.

CHAPTER 12

Back Home

THREE MONTHS LATER Somerled was approaching the fishing port of Mallaig, riding down from the higher ground which was shrouded in mist. He had in the intervening time, since making his vow in the castle garden, returned Piebald to Jock McIver, managed to earn some money, and been to visit his mother. He had found out that Jenny had another cousin on the Isle of Skye, and now pursued this as a wild hope.

He no longer sought Jenny to mend his own sorrow, but because he had sworn it; he felt the force of a religious vow. Having had insight into Jenny's own wound, he had seen the importance of forgiveness, and knew it was his duty to mend the heartbreak of another, the heartbreak he had caused. He had ever in the forefront of his mind the words of the old man at the fort, - "seek her out, open your heart to her and let God in." He had sworn before Christ in the flower-filled garden to never stop seeking her until forgiveness flowed. So he pursued Jenny now with religious fervour; in order to find a way of saying something to allow forgiveness to assuage the pain in her heart. He did it for her sake rather than his own; he did it because he genuinely loved her and wanted to heal her of brokenness and the bitterness of pain.

A sense of guilt in fact had newly entered his consciousness; he saw that the death of Roberta was entirely his fault. Deeply he had repented of his thoughtlessness; firstly in allowing his friend to be condemned instead of being on his side, secondly in so suddenly revealing it to his fiancé. He hadn't allowed enough care and thought to enter into his actions; he had blindly pursued his own ideals without care for the people involved. He saw it all now, aware of his guilty part in destroying lives. A new religious sensibility was the result; a sensibility which led him on a quest to remedy things as best he may, - by salving another's soul, and setting Jenny free.

Jenny had asked him in the letter she left to let her go free; but he wanted to free her in a deeper manner, which required seeking her out. He loved her now with a newly awakened soul. He wasn't the same; guilt had created a new Somerled, had carved out a thoughtful, deep character, - one motivated not by selfish passion but by a determined self-transcendence. His own mother noticed the difference in him.

"Mother!" he had called on entering the house, "Are you here?"

"Son, my son!" she cried, flinging herself at him and hanging round his neck. "Where have you been? I heard you went missing from the fort, that you mysteriously disappeared from the cell – what were you doing, son, where have you been?"

"I've been seeking Jenny, mother, trying to put things right."

"I said "you will rue the day" when you first met that lassie; I remember it well. We had had an argument. It was about your plans to go to France with Malcolm, and leave me here to pay the rent and manage the croft on my own."

"Yes I do remember mother. I remembered it in prison." He gave a shudder at the thought of that cold dank prison cell and his reckless intention of getting himself killed to exonerate his dead friend. But Malcolm wasn't dead, and he had found out from Jenny's father that he had indeed got to France.

He said nothing of the deep shudder this train of thought imparted to his feelings. He simply said "Here mother, I've brought some money. This will help pay the rent."

She opened the purse with apparent amazement and delight. "Where did you get all this?"

"Oh I worked for a bit, after I'd returned Jock McIver's horse in Durness," said Somerled with a son's typical reticence.

"But son, this is a small fortune."

"No it's not mother; it'll pay the rent." He paused, and saw her looking up at him as if hoping for the story which would more clearly reveal his adventures.

He sat down with a sudden sense of weariness. "I broke Jenny's heart, mother, and I've been trying to put things right. At first I thought dying to exonerate my friend would put things right, then I nearly killed myself out of despair, and I walked so very far in the wilds. Then Jenny's father took pity on me, telling me where Jenny was, and that Malcolm wasn't dead. Then I rode on his horse all the way to Fife to ask Jenny to forgive me. But she wouldn't, mother, she wouldn't" - - Here tears suddenly stung in Somerled's eyes –

His mother came close and wrapped her arms around him – "But I've made a vow, mother, to seek her out, and say something which will salve her wound." There was a pause before he exclaimed – "I've made such a mess of things, mother, I wish I could go back to that day I met Jenny, I was innocent then. And now I have guilt towering over my head, for indeed I caused the death of Jenny's best friend!"

"Son, I don't understand the half of this. You will have to explain it to me."

And so Somerled on that warm evening, whilst the wind whipped around their home and the water dripped in the eaves, told the whole story of his adventures to his mother, what had passed since that fateful day that he had met Jenny.

When he had finished, she on her part, having listened sympathetically with a mother's solicitude, said nothing. He openly wept, the tears coursing in the silence down his cheeks. There was no need to say anything, something deep having passed between mother and son.

Then, as she bustled around to put food on the table, for a mother's answer is usually to feed and nourish, she said very quietly- "you have no idea what is going on here, have you Somerled? You are rushing around, caring only for your Jenny and the assuaging of the griefs of the heart, whilst a great persecution is passing through all the land. Bad things are happening in the Highlands!"

The sorrow in the way she spoke struck him immediately, so that he raised his head as if cold water had woken him up. "What are you talking of mother?"

As she placed the warmed broth and oakcakes before him, it was now her turn to tell the tale. "Have you had your eyes closed, Somerled? After the defeat, king George's soldiers have plagued the highlands – it's Cumberland's men, - they call him the butcher- they terrorize the whole land, they take all our weapons – every dirk and claymore they can find- and burn the homes, and rape the women, and steal the cattle, and many young men they've carted off to work the plantations overseas. I tell you we are not even allowed to wear our own tartan plaid anymore. The whole country is direly suffering – there was Malcolm's mother down the glen – Don't tell me you have seen nothing of this?"

He laid his hand on hers in dismay; "Oh mother! What happened to Malcolm's mother?"

She replied hard-lipped; "it doesn't bear speaking of. But have you been blind to what is going on?"

Somerled was suddenly extremely aware of his blindness, his guilt, his overall sin. He had been mostly in the North, and the persecution had mostly happened in the Jacobite strongholds, but he was aware of his blindness. He had indeed heard tales.

"Mea culpa," he said under his breath. His mother asked what he said. "Nothing mother; I am very much aware these days of my blindness and my guilt; I was born blind it seems!"

"All of us are blind in our first innocence, son; we have our eyes opened by the experience of life. And sometimes it is painful."

"I've been so blind to others' pain," said Somerled miserably. Then a thought struck him, as he thought of the historical perspective of the time in which he lived; "But what of Bonnie Prince Charlie, the true king, what of him? I suppose he has been captured by now?"

"No; that's the strangest thing," said his mother with a brightness in her eyes, "he is still chased round the Western highlands, and wherever he goes they hide him. Even though there is a £30,000 bounty on his head, and he wanders like a hunted man, yet the clansmen never betray him, but are faithful and true."

"Faithful and true!" echoed Somerled, "Even though he made bad choices and lost at Culloden, and so many were killed, and now they get their homesteads burned and their clan-life destroyed! Aye they are faithful and true!"

His mother wasn't sure whether Somerled was speaking with irony at this point, but as their talk went on into the night, she saw that he was a true and faithful Jacobite if ever there was one! And it made her heart glad, and she felt consoled for his long absence.

He stayed a couple of days, did most of the heavy farm work that needed attention, and mended some of woodwork that needed mending. And as she became more talkative, his mother revealed something to him that he did not know; Malcolm's mother had a relative on Skye. Somerled turned this over in his mind; it meant Jenny too had a distant cousin on Skye; could she have taken refuge there? He knew Jenny was running away from him, but he sought her to do her good. It struck him forcibly that the true King was also in the area, and running away and hiding - - Could it be that their paths would cross?

Finally on a bright and sunny Autumn morning he saddled his horse and said goodbye to his mother, thanking her for opening his eyes to the reality around him, promising to come back soon. His path beckoned in front of him, calling him now to cross to Skye, with the hope that Jenny might be found there- "Jenny his own, Jenny his love," who was fleeing before his sorrow and his quest, and didn't apparently desire to be found.

CHAPTER 13

Beside the Loch

SOMERLED WAS NOW approaching Mallaig through the mist-shrouded mountains. He could hardly believe the sights he had witnessed on the way from his mother's house. Due to what she had said, his eyes had been really opened to the suffering of the Highland people around this area. What his mother had said, or declined to say about Malcolm's mother haunted him; there are worse things than death for a woman, and he sorrowed over her. He now saw evidence of the pillaging and burning of the crofts, thorough ransacking, and of the sorrow etched into the faces of these heroic highlanders. He mourned deeply for their plight.

He reflected how his eyes had been closed before, when all he thought about was his own emotional life, his Jenny and his pursuit of her. Suddenly the world had widened around him, and became full of people, real people, whose cry of desperation ascended to the heavens. He was changing rapidly; never the same Somerled, but always changed by grief, or guilt, or new-awakened sympathy. But somewhere among this sea of stricken humanity was Jenny, and he was determined to find her!

This enlargement of the sympathies of the heart was largely occasioned, made possible, by Jenny's rejection of his overtures in the garden. A different world opened up after that. He couldn't believe he was the same person who galloped in such naivety all the way from the northern coast to Fife, nor for that matter, that he could be the same Somerled who had first escaped from the fort with his stupidly concocted plan, nor the Somerled who had desperately fled and tracked across a wilderness. He was grown up now, he told himself, sitting easy on his high horse, and these things were done in the idiocy of his youth. But without his love of Jenny and the pain it caused him, he would never have transcended his boyhood. It was because, he reflected as he looked down on Mallaig, he had truly entered into the pain of another, seeing life through their eyes.

A boat was easily commandeered to ferry him across to the Isle of Skye, which from time immemorial had been the stronghold of the Lord of the Isles, the centre of their kingdom. The oars of the boat were soon plashing on the water, reminding Somerled of the silence and swish of the sea at Skerray harbour with Jock McIver, or amongst the lobster pots with Willy, the Fife fisherman. The sea always spoke deeply to Somerled, entering into his soul. This time he sat in silence, admiring the wildlife all around him, especially the otters near the shore, and the white-tailed sea-eagle, which soared majestically in the grey skies above. The sea was a swirl of grey to match the sky, but in the distance, the cloud-bank opened up and gave him a glimpse of the wild and magnificent mountain-range called the Cullins.

He had come here because his mother had mentioned that Jenny had a relative on Skye, and after searching all he could for three months, it was at present the only lead he had. But when they beached the boat near Armadale castle, the dash for pursuit entirely forsook him.

"What is the wildest spot on the island?" he asked the islander who had manned the boat, with an urge that struck out of the blue.

"Loch Courisk Sir," he replied, "it is the inland loch at the heart of the black Cullins; it is wild there and no mistake!"

"Can you take me there?" asked Somerled.

"I cannot Sir, as I must man the boat, but my father will. Yes, he can take you."

"If your father will take me, I will pay two gold sovereigns," said Somerled, feeling magnanimous.

"Oh Yes Sir," replied the boy, running off to fetch his father.

So soon, amid that wild and dangerous Scottish scenery, Somerled could be seen walking smartly along the mountain paths for a while and then picking his way painfully over the black Cullins toward the aforementioned loch. The elderly man who accompanied him seemed mystified as to why he wanted to do such a thing; Somerled himself was mystified by his sudden urge to experience true wilderness. Maybe he was trying to reconnect with those experiences he had in his wild state when he fled the fort and made for Durness. The solitariness and sheer beauty of those strange-shaped mountains had impressed him.

They walked for hours and the day was hot. Some autumnal mist swirled around the jagged peaks but on the whole it was a clear day, with dappled cloud and sunlight passing across the vast landscape. The black Cullins, with their jagged peaks and strange pinnacles of rocks, impressed themselves on Somerled's very soul. It was an arduous task, climbing so far, then edging their way along the cliff-face by the edge of the sea. Finally, after picking their way across a rock-strewn strip of land by a clear and tumbling stream, they arrived at the loch.

They both sat to rest, to recoup their strength. Somerled felt for a moment so deeply exhausted that he wondered how he would ever get back, it being now late afternoon. They sat in silence; as with his trips with Jock McIver or Willy the fisherman, Somerled knew all he needed to do was to listen, and experience what the place had to teach him.

It truly was a wild place; the loch was contained by the highest, most rugged mountains imaginable; it seemed to be held, cradled and contained by the very roots of the rocks of which the earth was made. There was a fierce wind whipping around Somerled, and despite that, with an ominous stillness, the surface of the water itself was placid and unruffled. He could hear the wind, but beyond that and carried by it was a complete and utter silence. It was so silent as well as so magnificently wild, that it quelled all his thinking. It was beyond thought; it was adamantine, ageless.

A white seagull breasted the wind, high up. Somerled saw it, and in that utter abandonment to the truly wild and ageless, he felt it sensibly as a harbinger of love, a sign that God's spirit was indeed present with him, like the spirit at creation hovering over the waters. A great longing rose within him, a cry of the alone to the Alone, a desire to live a life worthy of God's love - -

A short time later they were picking their way back to the shoreline of the sea; his experienced guide had asked him if he should point out the seals. They were hard to see by strangers who do not know where to look for them because they sit so well-camouflaged against the rocks. "There!" cried his guide, "And there, and there! See the baby pups!" Somerled's heart melted at the sight of these strange animals of the sea. He blessed them as they lay basking on the rocks in the small bay, and then sat meditatively for a short while, observing how all the rocks on the opposite cliff glistened in the fitful sunlight due to the water that coursed down them.

"Let us go now," he said after sitting thoughtfully, "I have a task to pursue, someone I need to find, who I hope is on this island."

"Who is it?" asked the man, willing to be helpful, "I know the names of every man on this island, so maybe I can point the way."

Indeed his guide could point the way; in leading him to the wildest part of the island, he had become friendly enough to be willing to help to the hilt, even though the islanders are a close-knit community, who do not give away their secrets easily.

He promised to write a letter of introduction for this smart young man of whom he had become strangely fond, and he invited him after this hard day of mountaineering to sup and lodge with them that night. Somerled was truly grateful because, though feeling happy, he was exhausted.

Late at night in the croft with the welcome bed, he looked out at what he could see of the mountains, and he could see the stars glinting above them. Strange, that he was there, right at the heart of them! And what had he known there? He thought again of the majestic rock, the still lake, the wind, and the strange silence. He thought of those moments when he saw the seagull winging its way above his head and hovering, - when his longing and yearning for God and for Jenny all became one.

And in that act of self-yielding to God, in the mysticism of the moment in the most wild of places, he had said to himself, "Jenny my own, Jenny my love, who belongs to God- I will reclaim you for God, for the forgiveness of God's love, - for which purpose I will strive to be worthy, for which at this moment I consecrate myself."

CHAPTER 14

In the Castle

IN THE MORNING the world looked different to Somerled. He felt cleansed and renewed after his excursion into the wilds the day before. The grass around the croft seemed to grow a brighter green and the sea not so far from the croft sparkled a deeper blue. He had sought Jenny for ages now and had felt tired, and terribly distressed by the oppression of the Highlanders that he saw all around him. But now he felt the beauty of the black Cullins had given a bath to his spirit, and the fact that he had consecrated himself to the purposes of God's love had reinvigorated him.

At the breakfast table, the homely old man who had been his guide, with his unkempt hair and copious beard, looked earnestly at Somerled and showed that he was willing to help to the hilt. "I'm lending you my only horse – you must bring it back mind – Ride to the North-west coast of the island- it is due West of Portree- and you will find Dunvegan castle. I have written a letter of introduction for you to someone called Ian McIver. I think he will have news of your Jenny, being kin."

Somerled couldn't thank the old man enough, realising how little the crofters had, and how it was rapidly being taken away from them by the English rule and their reign of terror. He gave assurances that, one way or another, he would return the horse. And thanking them profusely for their kindness and hospitality, he left, turning his horse to the North.

The horse wasn't as swift as other horses he had ridden, and nothing could match that amazing Piebald who had carried him swiftly form the far Northern coast to the Eastern kingdom of Fife. This horse was called Nancy, and plodded rather slowly. Hence at a slow pace Somerled tracked through the Red Cullins, leaving the Black Cullins to the West of him. He was amazed as the redness of their stone was warmly illuminated by the bright morning sun. It was an enchanting sight, and he enjoyed the ride, refreshed by a cool breeze from the sparkling blue sea on his right.

Finally, at the end of the day, when a damp evening mist was descending, he espied the finger of rock from between the trees which was Dunvegan castle. He dismounted and walked the last bit of the road, being very sensitive about approaching such an abode after the pain of what had transpired in that castle-garden in Fife. Supposing Jenny were really here? - his Jenny, looking from the windows?

As he rang the bell, which announced his presence with a loud clanging noise, his mind went back to the peculiar pain of that Fife garden, - how Jenny seemed astonished at the idea of forgiveness and had said that dreadful thing – "you are not the man I thought you were." The memory put Somerled off his purpose altogether, and disconsolately for a moment he turned away - - But the door was answered, and without saying a word, Somerled turned back and thrust the letter of introduction into the man's hand.

A few minutes later he was talking to Ian, the man he sought, in the entrance hall, the walls of which were coated with military hardware. It was a place where the visitor was forced to recall that life was about fighting battles, and loyalty to clan came above everything. Ian had told him he knew where Jenny was, when suddenly he looked up and gazed beyond Somerled, making a bow.

Somerled turned and saw a man coming down the steps. The man was dressed in ordinary highland garb, and he was extraordinarily handsome, with grey visionary eyes, and there was something about his bearing - - Instantly the truth flashed upon Somerled. - This was the man he had only glimpsed at Derby and Culloden - Bonnie Prince

Charlie! He remembered how he had foreseen at his mother's house that their paths would cross.

He fell on his knees; "my Prince, the true king!"

Graciously the Prince raised him and asked why he had come, and whether he brought news. "No news, my Lord" said Somerled, and he blushingly told how he had come to Skye in pursuit of his Jenny, who was once his bride- to-be.

"Far be it for me to interfere in affairs of the heart," said the Prince, smilingly, "I am busy myself fleeing from the English soldiers, and now I'm waiting for a French boat to take me back to France. That is why I came down, as I thought you might have news. But I can tell you what is in Jenny's heart."

"My Lord?" said Somerled, uncomprehendingly.

"Oh yes, I met your Jenny at Floddiegarry, after my brave Flora MacDonald took me over the sea to Skye. The thing is" – here he approached Somerled and threw an arm around him as if they were old companions, and his face expressed an earnest sorrow – "the thing is, she is broken-hearted."

Somerled for a moment felt bewildered, both by the man's closeness and by his statement. It made him remember vividly the conversation in the castle garden, when he had tried to explain what he had done to put things right, but Jenny had exploded with a pain and a bitterness which refused to forgive.

"The thing is," the prince went on, "women are peculiar creatures. They don't want to know what we have achieved or what we have done to put things right, they don't want to hear our boasts – didn't you know that, my man? What they want to hear is how much we love them. I gather you didn't explain that" - -

Somerled was dumbfounded, realising that Jenny must have confided thoroughly in this princely figure who now held him by the arm as if a comrade.

"I have had many travels," continued the Prince, "and what I've learnt in all of them is that what truly matters is true-heartedness. Yes, I've failed here, I failed when I turned back at Derby and I failed when I called for every man to seek his own safety at Culloden, and now I must leave these shores, a failure. But the loyalty I have seen, the true-heartedness of so many of my countrymen here, who would conceal me and do their utmost to save me, even with a high price on my head! This is the only thing that matters at the end of the day – true-heartedness!"

Somerled was amazed at the frankness of this man which he honoured, and the friendship he was extending to him in telling him all this. He was listening intently to what this true Prince had to say.

"She couldn't believe you could do such a thing, you know! You were hard-hearted to betray your friend and tell his woman in such a cold- hearted manner." - Somerled realised with a shock that Jenny must have told the Prince the whole story - "This is what matters to women- the heart!"

Somerled held his head down miserably. "I have changed," he said, "I'm not the man I was." He knew, as he said it, that it was very true.

"She needs to know that you have changed, that you are tender-hearted, and true-hearted. Shall I tell you what I told her? I told her that if her Somerled found her now, it was because he had long sought, and that is what mattered – true-heartedness!"

"Thankyou, thankyou," stammered Somerled, suddenly overwhelmed by how much potential good this man of the royal blood-line had achieved in his life. "How can I ever thank you?"

The prince beamed at him, glad maybe that he had successfully pedalled his own private philosophy. In a trice he was striding his way back up the steps, throwing his wise parting words over the astounded Somerled –

"That is what you have to do, - show Jenny you have a true heart!"

Somerled stood speechless for a while, looking up the staircase upon which the prince had vanished. It all made sense to him now. In the garden with Jenny he should have declared to her how much he loved her, like he did in Jock McIver's presence at Skerray harbour, instead of excusing himself, justifying himself, and boasting. But he had another chance, and hoped it would meet with success partly because the Prince had apparently told Jenny that his long-seeking of her proved true-heartedness. Yes, if Jenny forgave him now, it was because Bonny Prince Charlie had paved the way!

With a light-heartedness he didn't know he possessed any more, he parted from Ian, thanking him for the help he had been given at Dunvegan, - by royalty no less- knowing that he could now find Jenny at Floddiegarry. And he cantered out of the gardens, in which the flowers hung dripping with the wetness of the incoming mist, going as fast as the old horse could carry him. The promise before him was Jenny his own, Jenny his love, who only needed to know that he was changed from the man he was, and that he was true-hearted.

CHAPTER 15

At the Cottage

S O SOMERLED CANTERED away from Dunvegan in the thickness of the mist, and then he rode in the chilliness of the night through a landscape made wet with the sea-fret which was rolling across the island. He was oblivious of it, for he was only thinking how the true king had spoken to his Jenny as well about true-heartedness. He was excited because he felt this paved the way to his reconciliation with Jenny. All his thoughts were of Jenny, so that he didn't notice the rivulet running down his neck or the cold wetness of his skin.

When he reached Portree, the main fishing-town of the island, he realised immediately that he had a fever. Quite quickly he began to ache and shiver and his breathing became laboured. He found cheap lodgings for himself; there was nothing for him to do but to hole-up there until this ague passed.

For several weeks he lay ill in his bed, shivering fitfully, then coughing violently, and hardly ever eating. When he finally recovered, he looked a different man, with leaner cheeks, and ashen complexion. But he chose a sunny morning in December to set off on his quest once more, only and simply aware that he had consecrated himself to the purposes of God, to reclaim Jenny for divine forgiveness. He hardly thought any more of his own part in it; it was a sacred quest.

He had instructions how to reach Floddiegarry, where he hoped he could still find her. He rode past the Old Man of Storr, - that impressive bastion of rock that resembled a man's face, past the high pinnacles of rock, past the impressive limestone cliffs, and so down to the shoreline, to a bay by the edge of the sea. It was a blue-skied day, and this was reflected in the gentle-lapping blueness of the waves on the shore. He could see the hills of the mainland across the water; all seemed perfect and calm, -an idyllic day for such a high spiritual purpose.

Quickly he knocked on the door of the cottage; he didn't want to think how he might react if Jenny herself should answer. He had prepared certain words to speak, but he was so aware that what was said between them depended on the gift of the moment. It wasn't Jenny who answered, but he was shown into a cottage garden at the back, and there he espied her sitting on a bench under a tree, well-wrapped against the cool air. She appeared to be perusing a book in the sunlight. The garden flowers were not much to speak of at this time of year, but still the aspect of the garden reminded Somerled of that other garden where she had rejected his overtures and said that painful thing that still stung in his memory; "you are not the man I thought you were." But he was a much-changed man now; maybe she would see that.

He gently called her name so as not to alarm her. She looked up at him with only a mild surprise; she must have known that he still sought her.

"Why Somerled!" She gazed and him for a moment. "Why! you look thin and pale."

"I've been ill," he stated with simplicity.

There was silence between them, as each re-appraised the other. The fact that he had recently suffered illness did more than anything else could have done to touch the fount of her sympathies. Jenny too did not look the same; she was not the same carefree buxom girl of that idyllic summer of long ago; the extra years made her seem more mature and worn with care.

Somerled could tell things were not the same as in that Fife garden when he provoked such an outburst of pain from her, and she had fled from him. They were both at a different stage in their own lives, though still the same essential lovers. He remembered what the true Prince had told him; women don't like excuses or explanations, but simply declarations of the heart. He went up to her, sat beside her, and gingerly touched her hand.

"I make no excuses. There is no justification for what I did; I was hard-hearted and foolish. But I am not the same man Jenny, I am much changed. I am truly sorry," he declared, "believe me, I am truly! I never realised how much I hurt you."

Jenny's hand didn't respond to this, but they both sat in the silence, looking out across the sea.

"Jenny, I am not the same man I was; I have become devout, and sensible of others' suffering. Can you please forgive my younger self?"

There was still silence from Jenny; she was gazing at their hands, and slightly responded to Somerled's touch..

"I need you to forgive me Jenny. I don't ask because I deserve it, but because it will set us both free, and it is in your gift."

The silence continued, and Somerled didn't know how to interpret it; he continued to try and throw balm between them with his words. He remembered what the true Prince had told him; "show Jenny you have a true heart." It struck him, as it had done riding away from Dunvegan in the mist, that it could pave the way that the Prince had spoken to Jenny too.

"I am true of heart Jenny, or I wouldn't have sought you so hard and so long. This is what matters; trueness of heart."

Jenny held her palm to his in self-offering, and they enfolded each other's hands. He looked away from the sea to her face, and saw there were tear-drops on her long lashes.

It was at this moment that Somerled was stuck by another memory; what he had declared of his love of Jenny to her father in the boat at Skerray harbour. For he was searching for something to deeply touch her heart. Deep he searched into the past mist of his memory, till the words sprang to his lips:

"Jenny, I love you forever and always. You are like the air I breathe which I cannot live without; you are like the earth on which I walk and the bright canopy of the stars above. You are necessity to my very life; you are the best essence of myself, of my very soul. You are my bright star, my angel!" He paused, before he dared the final sentence; "If you can forgive me, I want to cherish you all of my days, and give you the best of myself, and make sure you are always happy."

There was a deep silence and you could have heard a pin drop. Somerled for a moment feared he had said too much. - -

Then Jenny burst into sobs and hugged him, snuggling her face against his breast just like she always used to do. "Oh Somerled, I do forgive you, I do!"

Somerled beamed with bright happiness; it was a pinnacle of intense bliss such as he could only achieve once in a lifetime. He let her sob in his arms, enfolding them gently around her and soothingly stroking her luxurious curls. "It's alright," he said "it's alright."

And he knew it was alright, - all was now right with the world and with their two souls now that he had won her forgiveness. He knew they needed to talk, to make clear and understand what had happened between them. But look, she was "Jenny his own, Jenny his love" truly once more, now that with a gushing release of the heart she had made that act of forgiveness.

CHAPTER 16

By the Hearth

"**I** FEEL BETTER NOW," declared Jenny. They were sitting in her room in the small cottage, and out of the window they could hear the swish of the sea, as it rattled the pebbles on the beach. They were warmed by the fire in the hearth.

Somerled sought for something spiritual to say, for now together with Jenny at last, his high religious fervour in seeking her seemed to be on the wane.

"Forgiveness releases from chains the one who forgives" he stated. But immediately he thought that too sonorously moral, and swiftly sat beside her to warmly hold her hands in his.

"I thought you would never find me," continued Jenny ignoring his statement, though she must have felt its truth, "I came thus far to get away from you. Yet in a sense I wished you would find me."

They both realised they needed to talk, to seek to understand what had passed between their two souls. When he had finally found her, mercifully he had said the right things, and the moment had come as gift. She had forgiven him with one swift swoop, but still explanations needed to be made, the time they had missed needed to be recovered, their own soul-stories understood.

"I met an old priest in the prison in Fort William," said Somerled, ready with his new sensibilities for this task of self-explanation. "He told me not to die to put things right, but to live and seek you. He told me you would be waiting for me."

"Yes I suppose I was. I'm sorry for my harshness to you at the house in Fife. I was having a hard time there you know, and you didn't help and you made the past seem freshly bitter."

"I understand. Sorry, I didn't say the right things."

"What purpose would your death have served?"

"Well I told a lie about the stealing of the money, in order to take the blame, and so clear Malcolm's name. It was like duty to the dead I suppose. I rather stupidly thought that it was way to earn your forgiveness."

"Oh Somerled, you weren't willing to die a horrible death, to get my forgiveness?"

"I'm afraid I was, though it seems rather childish now and a long time ago. After that I nearly died out of despair, when I walked through the wilderness on foot to your father's house, only rescued from it again by what the old man said to me."

"Oh Somerled!" cried Jenny, "you have been through such a lot on my account!"

"It doesn't matter Jenny; what matters is the state of our souls in the present. Besides which, I learnt that Malcolm isn't dead, but bides his time in France."

"I'm glad; I loved Malcolm." The affection with which she said it made a cold thought flashed into Somerled; the thought he had on the mountain-side that maybe it was Malcolm that Jenny really loved.

She saw the puzzlement in his face, and responded to it; "I mean I love him as a cousin. He didn't steal the gold did he?" she added pleadingly.

Somerled's brow contracted in consternation; he didn't have a clear-cut answer; "He did say to me when I caught him handling it, that there was a reason - -"

"But Somerled, why did you not trust your friend? How could you so betray your own belief in your own best friend?"

Jenny's question demanded an answer, and Somerled didn't have one. He wasn't at his best at the time of the trial, being so confused and hurt himself.

"And telling Roberta in the way you did! How could you let it so trip off your tongue that Malcolm stole the gold, as if it would have no consequences? They were about to be married, and you told her he was about to die a traitor's death; you said it as if it wouldn't matter to her!"

"Yes, it was a dreadful thing to do," said Somerled, hanging his head with the pain and the shame of the past. He was close to tears as he said: "I admit it; I lay the charge to my own immortal soul."

Jenny could see his heartfelt sorrow, but had to say it once more: "She is dead through your thoughtlessness, Somerled!"

Somerled finally let out a sob; "I'm so sorry Jenny!"

Jenny wrapped his head in her hands and pulled him to her breast. They both knew it was the end of the subject.

Then Jenny lifted his head and smiled into his face, and suddenly said "What do you think of the Prince? A brave man isn't he?"

Somerled could see there were tears in her eyes too, and she needed to change the subject. "He spoke to me about you" she confided.

"Yes I know; he told me." And Somerled clutched a handkerchief to his face.

"Yes we saw him over the sea to Skye. He was hidden by all the Highlanders you know. Despite the high bounty on his head, no-one would ever betray him. He told me that what mattered was true-heartedness."

"Yes, I know," he replied, slightly smiling at the philosophy the Prince pedalled everywhere; still, it had stood them all in good stead. The momentary amusement made him feel relieved from his emotional state.

There was silence between them for a while, as they cuddled affectionately.

"Do you remember when I first met you?" Somerled asked, "And do you remember what you first said to me?"

"Yes, I do. I said that you were a fine and handsome fellow, and in the height of being fully alive."

"And I was in that moment. And I am in this."

Somerled felt as he did in the past; gone was the religious idealism with which he pursued Jenny, back was the original physical passion.

They were intertwined now in a self-oblivious embrace; each only conscious of the other snuggled against their warm skin.

"Did you mean it Somerled?"

"Mean what?" he queried between his panting breaths.

"That you want to cherish me and make sure I'm happy; that you will give me the best of yourself?"

"I mean it. I said it truly." Somerled averred this in a kind of bright bliss, with his head buried in her thick black tresses.

"Come with me," she said, leading him by the hand.

And soon they sank into each others' arms, breathed into each others' souls, and consummated their love. Jenny his own, Jenny his love, Jenny who was finally, completely his!

CHAPTER 17

In the bedchamber

HE OPENED HIS eyes and perceived the low sunlight of a winter's morning slanting into the bedchamber. He listened and could hear the swish of the sea on the pebbled shoreline. And he heard the soft flow of breathing on the pillow beside him.

There lay Jenny, the inflow and outflow of her breath making her body softly rise and fall. He lay a hand on her soft white shoulder and caressed a filigree of her black hair with his fingers. He recalled with a sudden sweet sensation that moment when in the secrecy of the night she had utterly yielded to his embrace. It was like a sweet nectar which would last him the rest of his life.

He reviewed the previous day in his mind's eye. He dwelt fondly on that moment, which was really an eternal moment, when he had openly confessed his love to her, saying he would cherish her all of his days and give his best to her and make her happy, and she had uttered those words of forgiveness. And then again when she had asked if he had meant it and he had sworn it was truly said, and she had totally yielded to him. They were moments which would never pale but remain bright between them forever. He could live the rest of his life on the happiness of them. It was an earnest of God's own bliss.

He was content, - not the same man as the one who lay with her the night before, - not the man who was ever urged by a high quest, resolve, and urgent need to achieve forgiveness and union. He was content now as he lay back on the pillows, deliciously at peace.

Jenny turned half-asleep and whispered a name: "Malcolm."

Somereld's reaction was instantaneous: "did she say Malcolm?" Could it be that, as he had suspected all along, as he had seen clearly by the light of that sunset on the rugged mountainside, it was Malcolm who was her true love, and not himself?! His jealous suspicions about Malcolm were bad enough before, but now with the added emotional complexity which sexuality brings, it was like a poisonous lance straight into the heart! It was an intense sexual jealousy which reared its ugly head.

Suddenly Somerled regretted the loss of his high purpose, his spiritual resolve, his spiritual quest, his allowing of it to descend into common sexuality. As a man with upper parts of silver and gold, he didn't want to be reminded that he had feet of clay. He had attained sexual union with Jenny on the same day as achieving his consecrated goal of "winning her for God" through forgiveness. But sexual union hadn't been his aim, God knows it wasn't his aim! See the fallenness of human nature; in the chalice of bliss the poison; the canker at the heart of the rose!

He held his head in his hands and wept silent tears, - the tears of a man who had achieved his high aim, tasted ashes in the mouth, and was faced with a wasteland stretching in front of him. "What would he do now?" His purpose had collapsed, had been sullied at the height of its achievement, and he was left with a bitterness, an emptiness.

He realised he had loved Jenny most when she was unattainable, when he had forlornly pursued her; now that he had had her, had unmistakably possessed her, he found the passionate desire for her had waned. Perhaps it was ever thus with men - -

Lost in the convolutions of thought before Jenny was stirring, he now found no pleasure in the night before. He felt he had sullied his soul by giving way to sexual passion. He had betrayed his high calling, that consecration to the purposes and love of God that he had made at Loch Courisk. He had done something terribly wrong; he should have waited till their wedding night to love Jenny so that it would have God's blessing. He profoundly prayed for God's pardon - -
Again he was left, as the beginning of his story, trying to put right a mistake.

All this happened to Somerled before Jenny woke up. He had decided in the intervening time whilst the clock on the mantelpiece ticked away, that there was only one way to put right his terrible mistake; he would strive to be true to her, - to be true to that promise that he would cherish her all of his days, and give his best to her, and strive to make her happy. He had meant this with all of his soul, and now that they were married in the eyes of God, he would be true to his vow. Supposing she was got with child through their union? – he must save her from disgrace and difficulty. Yes, that's what he must do; marry her as quickly as possible, and honourably remain true to his vow.

By this time, Jenny had awoken, and greeted Somerled, who had an hour ago opened his eyes in bliss, and had since fallen into a mire of misery. "What's the matter Somerled?"

"We shouldn't have made love last night," he said gruffly, "it was wrong."

Jenny gave a gasp of dismay. "I thought it was what you wanted."

"No, I wanted something far higher, nobler, truer than that."

"Then why did you seek me?" enquired Jenny, perplexed.

"To set you free, by winning your forgiveness."

"But didn't you come to win me?" Jenny sounded confused and perplexed. "I gave all of myself to you" - -

"I know that; and I'm not blaming you."

Jenny, pained, fell into musing. "It's different for a man; my mother told me this. A woman gives all of herself at the same time, - body and soul interfused. But men, they separate their head from their heart, or their soul from their loins, and love-making is only a physical act which they rapidly regret." She rallied stoically; "But I don't regret it, and I never shall."

Somerled was hurriedly getting dressed, glancing at her as she talked. "It wasn't what I had in mind when I came here. You seduced me."

An electric shock went through Jenny at the words. She looked and saw the blank despair in his face, and spoke kindly; "No, I didn't Somerled; think about it" - -

Somerled was sorry for saying such a thing, and more sympathetically came to sit on the bed beside her. "Well how do you see it then?"

"Well from my point of view, I forgave you completely, and I gave myself completely, and it was all the same thing."

"The same thing?" he echoed, as if a brand new thought had entered his mind. He seemed struck by this, as if the novelty of womankind's experience had struck him anew and afresh. "Mmm!"

He continued making preparations about the room, as he revolved in his mind this new understanding of Jenny's perspective. He prompted her to get dressed, by announcing, "Come on we're leaving!"

A sudden doubt seemed to strike Jenny at his words; "Oh, you will look after me, and be true to me, like you promised?"

"Yes of course; I vowed to you truly, and will be true to it. I am true-hearted remember, like the Prince said."

"But I don't want to leave," protested Jenny, "I feel safe here."

"Soon it will not be safe anywhere," he replied grimly, "I am a man on the run and you helped the true Prince over to Skye. I heard the good news before I arrived here; he has escaped by taking a frigate to France. So the English wrath will fall upon all of us now. We'll get married on the mainland."

Jenny was overwhelmed by so much good news, her eyes widening and brightening; "Bonnie Prince Charlie finally safe in France? And we married?"

"Yes Jenny, yes, yes! Hasten now!"

He ringed his arms around her for a moment, and kissed her forehead. "Jenny his own, Jenny his love," Jenny whose life from this day, he knew, lay intimately entwined with his!

CHAPTER 18

By the Waterfall

A DEEP MISERY HAD settled on the Highlanders. Bonnie Prince Charlie may be gone, but in his wake followed endless oppression and killings and burnings and forced evictions. The clan system was being systematically destroyed by the English forces; their weapons and tartan were forbidden; not a tatter of their age-old honour was left remaining to them. Devastation lay in the wake of the second Jacobite rebellion of 1745; Scotland would never be the same again.

Three months later, from the day they hastily left Skye, Somerled and Jenny were on the run, pursued relentlessly by King George's soldiers from pillar to post. They had a secret source of happiness between them, but in their circumstances they suffered penury. They were now in the mountainous region of Moidart, having come down from the North, where they had been for the blessing of old Jock McIver, Jenny's father. This evening, after a spring day which saw the coolness of mist descending, they approached an inn near Ullapool.

Somerled avoided letting people know they were travelling as a couple, as he thought it safer. "Have you space for myself and this woman here- a relative of mine?"

"Your wife, Somerled!" piped up Jenny, "your lawful wedded wife!" She didn't want people to have any other thought but that she was his wife, and belonging to him.

Somerled turned to her; he knew her sensitivity on this point. He looked at his wife Jenny; still the same luscious hair, the dark expressive eyes, the pouting lips! Somerled was till very much in love with his wife.

"Forgive me!" he simply said.

He remembered as he said it how he had gone all across Scotland seeking her forgiveness, walking or riding with both an insatiable passion and a high ideal; he remembered the points on the journey, and the purity of purpose he required for the quest.

Now again, and often it seemed, the plea - "forgive me"! Since the hasty wedding, he had realised that forgiveness, both implored and bestowed, was a continual act, practised over a lifetime. He still needed daily to be forgiven for his thoughtlessness, his propensity to hurt the woman he loved.

The proprietor of the inn was suspicious now because of the attempted deception. He suspected the couple were hunted by the soldiers; to keep himself from involvement he refused to let them stay. Hence Somerled and Jenny for yet another night found themselves sleeping in one of the bothies of the region, without much shelter or warmth and without food. Things were becoming incredibly difficult for them; their married life was harsh.

In the morning they trudged on, though the freshness of the Spring morning was welcome to them, its beauty a consolation for physical hardship.

"I know we are both hungry and cold," stated Jenny, "let's talk to take our minds off it."

"What do you want to talk about?" asked Somerled

"Anything that has been occupying your mind." She said this with a woman's wily wisdom, for she knew something had been occupying her husband.

Suddenly it tumbled out of Somerled; "Explain to me why you mentioned Malcolm's name when we first woke in bed together, - at Floddiegarry, you remember?"

"Did I? Well I must have been dreaming about him." There was a silence between them as they picked their way through ferns and heather.

"After all," Jenny went on, "he was my favourite cousin, and we were very close that summer. And I spent a lot of time with him, you know, and his mother, when you weren't there." A thought struck her; "you are not jealous, Somerled, surely?"

"Yes, I suppose I am," said Somerled gruffly. "How is it that the keepsake I gave you ended up in his possession?"

"I don't know about that, but I swear to you, there was nothing between us save the affection of cousins."

A shout went up, a soldier's cry. The innkeeper must have betrayed them; he probably did it for money. They could see the red-coated soldiers approaching them from a distance, laden with their weapons.

"Run, Jenny, run!"

Though they ran as fast as they could, Somerled was slowed by Jenny, and when they came to a narrow gorge, where a waterfall plummeted deeply into a dark hole, whose bottom could not be seen due to vegetation, the soldiers had rapidly caught up with them. The place was called the Falls of Measach.

They crossed a narrow footbridge over the gorge, and then on the opposite bank Jenny twisted her ankle and fell heavily onto the heather. "I can't go on" she cried out her husband. "You must leave me and flee."

"Jenny I can't leave you" he replied, sinking to the ground by her side.

"You must!" she urged, "they will not kill me, a defenceless woman, but they will most certainly kill you."

"I'm not leaving you, Jenny my own, Jenny my love."

"They are coming. I hear their feet. You must flee!"

"Never mind Jenny. Look at me, talk to me – we may only have a few minutes together. Oh Jenny, I'm sorry!"

"What for, my dear one?"

"For not finding you sooner, and for giving way to my passion when I did find you. And for not trusting you. I've had this jealousy all this while."

Suddenly a shot rang out from a soldier's musket; Jenny was hit, full in the chest, yet she went on talking to Somerled as if she hadn't felt it and it didn't matter. She was oblivious to all else as she spoke the fullness of her soul to her husband:

"Oh my own, my love" she sweetly stated, "it's only to you that my heart has been wedded, and only love of you has possessed me. There was only you, it was only ever you!"

On saying that, she suddenly went limp. Somerled realised she was dying in his arms; the wet blood form the wound trickled from his fingers. He shook her and called her name. She simply whispered "I want to sleep," and breathed her final breath.

Somerled clutched her to himself and rocked back and forth, his head buried in her thick hair. He looked up, hearing the soldiers searching for the footbridge. He saw a rainbow arched in the spray of the deep-delved waterfall.

It suddenly struck him, - this was the iconic moment which had for so long haunted his dreams and waking thoughts; the moment by a waterfall with his head in Jennys' thick black hair, and there was the rainbow, right there!

But his face was buried in the tresses of a dead woman, - the dead body of his beloved wife, - rather than rapture it was an abyss of pain. Was all of his life heading towards this moment of desolation and loss? He let out a cry of endless anguish; he howled in his pain.

This was the end of all Somerled's dreams, his pursuit of Jenny, his high calling to win her forgiveness; now he was left with her dead and lifeless body in his arms.

Suddenly he knew what he had to do. He would be killed anyway when the soldiers caught him; he was already condemned to die the death of a traitor, his life already forfeit. After a last clutch of Jenny's body to his heart, he let go, and took a running leap into the dark and craggy hole into which the water thundered.

And as he plummeted, he breathed the dear and familiar words, - "Jenny my own, Jenny my love" - - - whom he would join in death's embrace.

"For Love of the Moors"

Emily's Story

A DISCLAIMER

*This is **not** an autobiography, but a story I have imagined. I have drawn upon my own memories of Yorkshire and Austria, but this is Emily's story, not mine, and what happens to her did not necessarily happen to me.*

CHAPTER 1

Falling

S HE LABORIOUSLY CLIMBED the last of the steep ascent, the wet fir-fronds whipping round her ankles as she trod the springy heather, till finally she sat on the sturdy outcrop of rock at the top – the strange flat rock, doodled on by prehistoric man with strange cup-like hollows and spirals. She quite readily got her breath back, being young and fit, then breathed deeply the wind which whipped on this Yorkshire Moor, and surveyed with pleasure the wide scene below her.

Beyond the wildness of the fir-fronds and heather, the small town of Ilkley nestled in the strange mixture of greenness and grime which was Yorkshire in the 1960's. The generous farmland stretched in emerald glory up into the far distance, whilst in the nearer town which nestled against the moor, she could see the many chimneys belching out smoke from what seemed toy brick houses far below. She wished the smoking houses were not there, spoiling the pristine character of her beloved homeland, her playground, her Yorkshire. But best of all of course were the moors, and she turned her body to look into the wild tussle of elements and growing things which was Ilkley Moor. She stood up and threw her arms out, as if to embrace the wind. Then with head thrown back she incanted –

What hath those lonely mountains worth revealing?
More glory and more grief than I can tell;

> *The earth that wakes but one human heart to feeling*
> *Can centre both the worlds of heaven and hell!*

The words were Emily Bronte's of course, who walked through life in close communion with the Yorkshire moors, - Emily her namesake, -

Emily so much like me! I wonder if my mum knew when she named me that I would be like her in character? I wonder if all Emilys are similar? Or maybe it's that you grow to be like your name? What does my name mean? I must find out. I'd never thought of that before; maybe you grow to be like your name, and that it is God's destiny that you turn out like that. Is that a silly thought? If it's true, think what a responsibility mothers have! Maybe there's something in it.

She turned around suddenly, as she perceived that she was not alone, and that she was not solitary in her thoughts, which she suspected she may have spoken aloud, as she often did.

"Ee by gum, if it ain't a raw day! Are ye on your own up 'ere, luv?"

Why can't people leave me alone? You come all the way up here, walking for three hours since breakfast to be alone, and there's a person here to bother you!

She endeavoured to answer politely, but making it clear she wasn't willing to stop and talk trivialities in such a wild and beautiful natural arena.

"Yeah, it is a cold day, though I don't mind; I prefer it to being hot when walking. I'm just moving on, if you don't mind."

With a nod of her head toward the stranger, who looked like a local, complete with backpack and walking stick, come for a daily constitutional from a town nearby, she gathered herself to set off walking into her favourite destination, - the inner wildness of the moor.

Perhaps he does mind, that I won't stay and talk, but I won't for all the tea in China! I don't like the look of him; Aunt is always telling me to keep myself safe where strangers are concerned. It's not the safest thing in the world, walking the places I walk on my own, I don't suppose. Why can't there be nobody here but me? You would think with all that space they have in the towns! Mind you, I suppose it's a different kind of space than there is *up here - - Still, I consider this to be <u>my</u> space! And as such, no-one has the right to accost me here! A damned cheek, that's what I call it!*

She turned for an instant, to check that the man was moving away, and not following her! She had had instances before of being followed in lonely places, and though she never told her Aunt about it, it had been frightening. It seemed okay, as the hiker was following the line of the ridge, so she breathed a sigh of relief.

The thing is, why can't people leave me alone! Why can't my family leave me alone, instead of nattering at me and oppressing me, and always telling me to do things? Why can't my teachers leave me alone, instead of complaining that I'm late because I was looking at the flowers, or shouting at me for gazing out of the window at the blue sky? Why Oh why can I not find a home for the heart where I can have enough solitude, enough chance to be silent and listen to the sounds of nature around me, and enough time to say all I want to say uninterrupted to the God I believe lives at the core of me? I'm not asking much, am I? Am I? Am I?

Her inner voice chimed with the wild cries of the birds which inhabited the heather. It was getting boggy underfoot now; as always she was rushing forward, feeling angry and head-down, and not noticing that she was stumbling straight into a bog. She looked around, studying the lie and look of the grass and heather and tufts of moor-flowers, to see if she could find a way out. Or the way that looked most promising. She decided which way to go, whilst remaining rather clueless.

An hour later she was muddy up to her knees, and her hiking boots had stuck to her squelching woolly socks, as she ploughed onwards through boggy terrain looking for safe landmarks. She felt desolate in the core of her, worn out and cold; and she was all alone, and apparently lost.

How can I be lost up here, on the moor I know so well? Gosh, if I'm lost here I can be lost anywhere! Imagine the potential for getting lost as you go through life! You are just walking happily along and suddenly wham! you're in it and mired up to your knees! It reminds me of that "slough of despond" in Pilgrim's Progress!

She smiled to herself as she remembered the pleasure of reading Bunyan's classic book of a Christian's struggle, whilst with a torch under the bedclothes last night. Her aunt had shouted to her as usual, "Time to switch the lights out luv" – but she had some while ago found a means to prevent this enforced bed-time and secretly bought a small torch. Even what she spent her money on was watched, but she wasn't watched out here, and that was part of the reason she loved the place.

Ultimate freedom, this is what the moor is to me, - even the freedom to get stuck in a bog!

"Ee-up luv! D'ye need any help!" It was the cry of the man whom she thought she had left way behind; the man who had caused her to march away cross and with her head down in the first place, hence making her lost. She felt confused; her instinct was to run away. The strange man with the back-pack and walking stick, with an elderly screwed-up face and balding head, was standing to the right and back of her. She looked at the tussocks of grass to the left, - they were greener and more promising, looking firm and springy, - she had often jumped from tussock to tussock across a wet area and never fell in. She took her aim and launched herself. Her usual sure-footedness failed her - -

I'm falling! - -

CHAPTER 2

Suffocating

WHEN SHE CAME in the door, she was immediately scolded by her Aunt.

"What have ye done to yeself! What's happened to ye! Just look at ye! Ye're covered in mud – it's caked so thick I can scarce see ye'r legs!"

She limped painfully across the threshold. Her ankle had been strapped by the hospital in Ilkley after she had fallen and sprained it badly. She'd had no sympathy from the nurses, and now was getting no sympathy from her aunt. The only person who had been kind to her in this minor catastrophe, and affront to her dignity as a seasoned hillwalker, was the strange elderly man with the crinkled face, who had gingerly balanced his walking stick as he bore her weight and limped to a safe rocky place, out of the bog, leaving her to sit whilst he went to get help. The ambulance had then come from the nearby road, and bound her ankle before carrying her down. She had meanwhile sat for ages, deep-plunged in misery, endlessly revolving in her thoughts:

How can I go back like this?

The stranger whom she was at first wary of, called Ernest, had been in the end quite kind; she had promised to meet up with him next week in Otley when her ankle was improved; even though painful, they had said it was sprained, not broken! Meanwhile she had to face her aunt.

"I've hurt my ankle aunt; I had to go the Ilkley A&E."

This news did not, as she hoped, promote her aunt's kindness, her coming forward and making much of her. If anything, she became more cross.

"I'm proper narked with ye! I told ye it would happen one day! I've told ye time and time again; ye can't just go wandering across the moors."

By this time Emily was in the sitting room and collapsed wearily onto an armchair, noticing how she couldn't see the fire for all the wet washing that was piled round it on clotheshorses. Of course it was Monday, washing-day! She put her leg up gingerly on the sofa, wincing momentarily at the pain, with a resigned look of patience painted all over her face. She already knew the gist of the criticism that was coming.

"Why can't ye be like other young girls of your age! – Going out to dances, going out with boys, going to the cinema! Why, Oh why Emily do you have to moon around writing poetry, looking at flowers and walking across the moors! What possesses ye! I didn't do that in me own young days! 'Taint natural!"

Please Aunt, leave me alone!

The voice came screaming into her head, but she sealed her lips. She'd had suffered too many arguments with her aunt, which she never won, and now she felt tired and pained. She felt very tired - - the next thing she knew she was asleep.

Aunt Bessie was left peering down at her, a girl on the way to womanhood, looking half like a baby and half like an angel, with her rich and wavy dark-brown hair tossed around her face.

She had long and delicious dreams, - the kind of dreams that go on and on forever and are sweet and refreshing. She had been in a place where big things went on and on, enchanting her, - big skies, big seas, big mountains.

My Gosh, the mountains! Could such mountains possibly exist! They were like fingers of rock jutting complex pinnacles into a lucid blue sky! Imagine walking across those rocky peaks! But surely no such thing existed!

It was the smell of rhubarb pie which slowly wakened her.

She sat up suddenly, the sudden twinge in her ankle reminding her of the day's calamitous events.

"Oh Aunt, you've made my favourite pie!"

"Aye luv! You know what I think about rhubarb – best rhubarb in't world is grown in Yorkshire! I like to think on it, just growing there in the dark in our fertile Yorkshire soil! And ye'self too will be growing in our Yorkshire soil and Yorkshire air, whether I mind it or no, as is the natural way of things. Anyways, I just nipped down to the greengrocer to get some for yer tea."

Emily was suddenly overcome by her aunt's kindness and burst into tears, whilst her well-bosomed aunt put her arm round her.

"Nay Emily don't take on so; everything'll be alreet in the end, ye'll see!"

Emily felt sorry that she had argued with the woman who had taken the place of her irreplaceable Mum, and then realised that actually she had kept her silence, and hadn't argued back at all. It was now that she felt fresh and fit for arguing.

"I wish you wouldn't go on at me! I've told you before I've no interest in boys! I'm seeking something else."

"But what luv, what?! All yer Uncle Arthur and I want is that you should finish yer schooling, find a nice boy and settle down - -

"But I don't want that aunt, can't ye understand!"

"Well what do ye want Emily?"

"I want, I want, - -

I want to get away from this place, I want to get away from the mill-towns of Yorkshire with their grime, away from the dirty foggy air, and away from the way you are suffocating me. I want endless space, endless moors, some place where I can be free, where I can breathe, where I can be myself.

"Well what do ye want Emily? Ye have to learn to settle down and be happy here, ye have to take Yorkshire as ye find it!"

Despairingly she fixed her eyes on the faded wallpaper opposite and the dark oak sideboard with the heavy Bush radio standing on it. She felt the walls were closing in on her.

"No - - No, I'm different! I want to go somewhere else, be somewhere else -"

"Folks don't just waltz off and leave their home behind, girl. Where is there to go? Think on it luv!"

"I don't know, there must be somewhere."

"These are wild dreams luv, wild dreams! I ken ye were upset when yer parents died, and ye didn't feel at home with us at first, but ye have to settle down, ye have to accept things as they be!"

Something in Emily's head screamed, for a raw nerve had been touched.

No, no! I started on my quest when they died, and I'll never cease, - not till I find what it is I'm searching for! Never! I know it will drive me into strange places, over mountains, and into danger - - but I have to search, I have to go, because it's not to be found here! This isn't my home here, the place where I can rest!

"Emily!" Her aunt was shaking her shoulders, worried about the glazed look which had come across her face. They had once sent for a psychiatrist, concerned about these strange bouts, when she didn't seem to inhabit her own body.

"Come on girl, be sensible!" she cajoled, as she heard the kitchen door open and sneck close again. "Look, I hear yer uncle Arthur in for his tea!"

"No, I'm going up to write!" declared Emily, breaking away, knowing she would soon be sitting solitary in her bedroom with her head in her hands.

You make me feel that I can't breathe!

CHAPTER 3

Daring

THREE WEEKS LATER and the first snow of the winter had fallen. It lay momentarily crisp and white on the rich Yorkshire grass. This morning Emily was attempting to go to school for the first time without her crutches, though she still used a stick, to help keep the weight off her sprained ankle.

She loved her school; it aimed high at encouraging the most intelligent pupils, being a grammar school, and in her studies Emily often felt herself stimulated and fulfilled. She was often in most subjects the brightest in the class. She was usually taken two-thirds of the way there by her Uncle Arthur, in his little Ford Popular, because the mill in which he played such a dominant role was situated nearby. Unfortunately this meant she was singularly subject to his bad temper every morning, her Aunt and cousins still being a-bed.

"Will ye hurry up Emily!"

"Alright, I'm coming, I'm coming!" She rammed another flapjack in her mouth, and took another sip of the hot milk that she liked to have with honey, before she grabbed her school-bag. She had a theory that taking hot milk instead of coffee freed her of the headaches she was often afflicted with; it was a kinder way of waking the brain up in the morning.

When she had jumped in the car, the windows instantly steamed up because of the raw cold air. Even here there was no let up from the unrelenting barrage of inhibitions she felt her uncle aimed at her.

"Stop breathing Emily, ye're steaming up the winders!"

Now I'm not even allowed to breathe! What will come next! I just wish I were free and far away!

Finally they got there, and she was glad to walk away from the mill car-park, away and free from her uncle's presence. She quickly found the little patch of green grass on a banking, with the small lone tree in the middle, where she always liked to pause and ruminate. This morning she was allowed the treat of seeing her footsteps imprint themselves in the fresh white snow, which was so fine a layer it covered the grass almost like a thick frost. She turned, to see with pleasure her little row of lone footsteps, as the weak sun struggled from behind a cloud, and sent a shimmering sparkle into the imprints.

Wow, look at that, it's lovely! Reminds me of Good King Wenceslas! I wish it could stay like this. I know full well that in the space of an hour this white snow will be covered by a layer of soot and grime from the dirty air. It's always like that; Yorkshire is such a dirty place! Look, I can see it from here; every chimney from every row of houses belching out smoke, let alone the black stuff from the mill chimney! Well this is the way it is I suppose; it will never change; Yorkshire is the centre of the woollen trade, and that's that!

She went up to the little lone tree and examined the remnants of withered dry leaves on its branches. She sighed unhappily; she was thinking about her uncle.

It's not that I dislike my uncle; he's a kind enough man in his way, and it was good of him and my Aunt to take me in after the accident, but I wish he would stop shouting at me. I can't seem to do anything without him shouting at me. Mm, I remember this little tree in the spring when I found colourful snowdrops round its roots. And I cupped them in my hand and thought of Blake's poem:

> *"To see infinity in a grain of sand*
> *And heaven in a wild flower*
> *Hold eternity in the palm of the hand - -"*
> *Look at the time!*

Glancing at her watch she realised that once again she was going to be late for school. She had been ticked off for this so often; she had better run - -

"Ye must stop dawdling on the way to school Emily; ye must stop mooning about, looking at trees and flowers! And we don't want ye visiting this Ernest-chap in Otley on Saturday!"

Emily inwardly groaned that most of what her Aunt said seemed to be criticism and carping. She breathed deeply trying to gather courage for an answer.

"Look Aunt, it was Ernest who saved me from a far worse fate on the moors. If he hadn't come along, with a sprained ankle in a bog, I could have been out there all night, - I could have even died out there. He really did save me, give him credit! I'm only going to thank him!"

She had cleverly avoided saying anything about the poor attendance at school, which so narked her Aunt. The subject was passed over, as she focused attention on the subject which was causing even more contention.

"I'm just asking ye child, why are ye showing any interest in an old man, when ye pay no attention to boys of ye'r own age?"

Not this again! I feel I'm going to scream! It's like being constantly challenged- why are you not normal? I may not be normal by their lights, but I just think I'm special. Maybe it's because of my Mum and Dad being so suddenly taken away from me- I remember that day, that dreadful day when I came home from school, the awful shock - -

"Emily!" Her Aunt was shaking her by the shoulders, alarmed by that glazed look in her eyes again.

"I'm sorry, were you saying something?"

"I give in" groaned her Aunt, "Ye just go, I'll say nae more about it!"

So two days later, on the Saturday morning, Emily was travelling on the bus to the neighbouring town of Otley, clutching her small parcel of chocolates and dates, feeling apprehensive.

I remember I didn't like the look of Ernest at first, in fact I rather ran away from him. But he turned out to be a kindly old man at the last and he looked after me well; just goes to show you shouldn't judge a book by its cover. His wife sounded nice on the phone. I do hope it goes well; I'm just longing to find someone who will understand me better - -Aunt Bess and Uncle Arthur don't understand me at all.

For a moment her thoughts flitted to the faces of her Mum and Dad; her grief over their deaths was still too fresh for her to reflect on their memory. Just for a moment they were present in her thoughts until she flinched away from the pain; the accident had been an anguish to her young impressionable soul. It had been the day she had started her journal and written her first poem:

My eyes are brimful of tears, my heart is heavy as lead
And my very soul is crying out for love and understanding - -

She shook herself as tears brimmed in her eyes, her grief as raw as ever. She made herself think instead of the gratitude she felt when her Aunt and Uncle, with their Maggie and little Fred welcomed her into their home. Maggie at present would be working in Woolworth's at her Saturday job, little Fred playing in the crescent, the two parents preparing to go shopping in Bradford. And here was she, doing something daring and extra-ordinary, hoping she would find the empathy she craved in a man old enough to be her grandfather.

I'm rather scared; do hope it goes okay!

CHAPTER 4

Trusting

EMILY HAD PURCHASED a bunch of flowers from Otley market before she stood on the doorstep with her heart in her mouth. A lady opened it who looked a bit waspish, as if unhappy at this visit from a young girl.

Emily attempted to hold out her hand graciously, saying "Hello, I'm Emily, I've brought flowers for you, I've come to talk with your husband; he rescued me on Ilkley Moor."

The wife's face brightened as she took hold of the flowers; "That's proper kind of ye; ye'd best come in to the best parlour."

They passed through a kitchen, where a real fire was roaring in the grate, and a pressure cooker was boiling on the range; the room smelt faintly of boiled cabbage. It was an old house, Emily noted, one of those back to back terraces originally built to house mill workers. It brought to mind the home of her grandparents, who had passed away when she was very young. The posher room they passed into felt damp, and smelt of old furniture and mothballs.

Suddenly, to her relief they were greeted by Ernest, who clasped her hand and cheerily stated, "Nay, wife, nay, we'll sit in't kitchen by our cheery fire. Ye won't want to bide in this dark room, will ye lass?"

Emily felt a grateful sense of relief, partly at the thought of sitting by the fire, and partly at his warm friendliness.

As she was stretching out her hands to the fire and cradling the cup of tea on her lap which his wife Jane provided for her before disappearing upstairs – "to do the bedrooms" as she said – Ernest turned to her with a bright and compassionate look on his face:

"So what has brought ye lass to me door? To tell truth, I doubted after I got ye to't hospital to clap eyes on ye again!"

"I just want to talk," admitted Emily, "to tell the truth, I feel my family really don't understand me. I'm grateful for having Aunt Bessie and Uncle Arthur, - they've been very kind to me since my own Mum and Dad passed away, - but they are so far from understanding me, and I feel so alone!"

"Aye, it's a rum do lass, when we find ourselves without the understanding of those we bide among! I'm real sorry to hear ye are so unhappy, but don't be maungey, mayhap I can say sommat to cheer ye!"

Emily was suddenly close to tears because of the offered sympathy. "Do you think you can?"

"Well tell me all, and I'll give it a bash."

She launched into the long tale of how happy she once was, and then all about the car accident, which had suddenly taken her parents from her, - she related the anguish of the day she came home from school to be left reeling by the news – She went onto say how she had sworn to find meaning in it all, how she had set off on her inward voyage, reading about Eastern religions, and mulling over poetry books, and wandering around admiring nature and writing her own poetry. But her Aunt and Uncle had thought this unnatural for a young girl, and wanted her to have boyfriends like other teenagers. And so she had been left misunderstood and solitary, then she positively sought to be solitary, as it seemed to be less painful. And above all she peppered all her tale with the reality of her deep and abiding love of the Moors, and how she spent so much of her time there. "Is there something wrong with me?" she ended plaintively.

"Ee by gum lass, there's nothing amiss with that! Why even meself did similar things in my youth! Ye see all these books on that shelf over in't corner, I read all them in me youth, even though I had to work in't mills to earn a crust - self-taught ye know, self-taught!"

Emily placed her empty cup on the solid table, which was covered by a thick blue woollen cloth and went over to look at the books. She opened one of them and found each page covered by pencil markings.

Why there's the complete works of Shakespeare, Wordsworth, Shelley, Keats here,- he surely can't have read all these! I took him for a kindly old chap who walked the moors, and he's clever enough to have educated himself- -

She must have voiced her amazement in her reaction, for he beamed at her, boasting, "Yeah, read 'em all, and studied 'em, studied 'em reeght well!"

"Have you ever written poetry yourself?" She asked, suddenly really curious.

"That I have lass! Maybe when ye next cum, ye can show me sum of ye'r poetry, and I'll get out sum of me own."

Yes I should like that!" she eagerly replied.

"Tell me why ye roam the moors so much? What de ye find a-top there?"

"Well I so much hate the noise and the busy-ness of the traffic and the dirtiness of the air, and I can never breathe very well with the fog – I had to wear a fog mask at the junior school – and I hate the mills, belching out the fumes."

"It's no use hating the mills lass: without mills there'd be no Yorkshire!"

"I know Yorkshire has been built on the woollen industry," replied Emily "but does it have to be so smokey and dirty?"

"Aye lass, 'appen it does!"

"But on the moors, the air is clear, and you can see for miles, and breathe it in, and it's wild and free, and you can just roam to your heart's content, and think and feel what you will, it's - - liberation!"

"Aye, 'appen it's liberation, as ye put it" he said echoing her long word, " but ye can't bide up there to earn ye're keep. Meself I came through the hard times of the thirties, and we were glad to be able to work in't mills, even though we got our wages as vittles in wheelbarries!"

She started at the novel thought; "What! you got food in wheelbarrows instead of your wages!"

"Aye lass, and glad of it too! Them were hard times!" His face looked sad.

He suddenly glanced at the clock which was ticking loudly on the mantelpiece and poked the fire which was now dying down to a red glow of coal; she was suddenly conscious she had been there quite a while, engrossed.

Then the man whose face she had grown to trust spoke his opinion: "I ken things don't seem reeght for ye, lass, and ye sense the world is about to tumble round ye're ears, but" - - there was a pause as his face contorted and he struggled for words - -"but just ye trust, and all shall be well."

"But how?" responded Emily.

"I'm not sure I ken just this instant – it's a mystery!" His face shone serene, as though he were completely confident.

A sudden sense of new hope bounded within Emily's breast. *Can this kindly and wise old man give me hope, solve my problem, show me a way forward? I trust him, yes I trust him - -*

Soon outside the door and on her own, having bid farewell, her mind simply surged with happiness. *There's someone on my side at last; I'm not struggling all alone; someone understands!*

CHAPTER 5

Perceiving

LITTLE FRED SUDDENLY let out a scream. His mother ran into the other room where he had been left to do "cutting out," to create a montage of dinosaurs; a gush of blood was welling from his forefinger.

"Oh Freddie I told you to mind with them scissors!" She held him to her breast, pressing the wound with a hankie, fussing over him.

At that moment Maggie came in; she had been trying on skirts upstairs which she had bought in Bradford after doing her Saturday job. She was two years older than Emily, and a vain young woman, so unlike her cousin. She walked in, swishing her skirt around, which was a similar colour to the jumper she had bought the week earlier. Emily looked on enviously, as she didn't have enough pocket-money to allow her to buy new things.

"You look beautiful, me lass!" commented Uncle Arthur as he glanced up from his newspaper. Emily had noticed that he always called her "my lass" in a tone of affection, but never herself. Still that was to be expected, seeing she was only a second-best niece.

Maggie took some more twirls around to show off the long turquoise material, - she had harboured a longing for a long skirt because she had been admiring the skirts of the pioneer women in the Westerns.

"That's enough!" commented Aunt Bessie, disapprovingly, "Stop trying to earn more admiration from yer father!"

"What I can't understand" replied Uncle Arthur, "is how with a father as mill supervisor, she hasn't got a better idea of co-ordinating colours!"

And is that the only thing she gets wrong? How is that Fred and Maggie are so well accepted, and admired and fussed over, and if I get any attention at all, which isn't often, it's all carping and criticism? Really, I just feel unloved and unwanted.

"I just want to ask about tonight - - "

"Not now Emily," grumped her uncle, "I want to do the football pools."

When he had left the room, she helped her aunt get the first aid kit out and bind the little boy's finger with a bandage; she was good at knots, having been taught by her father. Her Aunt used the opportunity for a serious talk.

"He hasn't touched ye has he Emily? Ye know, kissing and the like!"

At first Emily couldn't think what she was talking about. Then blood surged through her head with acute embarrassment.

"Of course he hasn't Aunt; don't be ridiculous!"

There was an awkward pause and silence, as Emily thought with fondness of the elderly man with the very expressive face, who had given her such hope.

"He's just a nice, kind, wise, old man" she protested.

"But Emily, he's old enough to be yer grandfather!"

A sudden reserve of anger and rebellion flared in Emily: "For heaven's sake, leave me alone!"

She flounced off, up to her room again. Her aunt came to the bottom of the stairs and called after her; "Remember to come down for yer tea; it'll be on't table this half-hour."

I have to get away from this family; they so oppress me. They don't understand that there is more to life than the things they are obsessed about; can't they lift up their heads for once? - - I'll write poetry - -"I met a dream the other night which told me of despair; then an angel clad in white rent the darkened air" - - She busied herself writing a poem about Christmas, to keep her mind off her troubles.

Thus began the evening when they went together as a family to the Yeadon cinema to see the newly- out "Sound of Music." Here was a rebellious young woman similar to herself revelling among the Austrian mountains; it revolutionized Emily's worldview. - -

The next Saturday, like a shot she was round to the house in Otley to talk with Ernest; her Aunt had not been able to prevent her.

"Have you seen the Sound of Music?" she blurted out, as soon as they were in the kitchen by the glowing hearth. She could hardly contain her excitement.

"I've heard a deal aboot it," he said, "ye can tell me yeself what 'appens; meself ah daynt go see films much!"

"But it's marvellous, you must go see it!" Emily's enthusiasm was spilling over; she was a picture of young eagerness.

"Well on ye go then! Tell me aboot it!"

"Well there's this girl who's a nun, and she's rebellious and won't obey the nuns and it starts with her singing on a mountain-top – "

Twenty minutes later, having been told all about the film, and been treated to snippets of the songs, Ernest leaned back in his armchair, and lit his pipe with a taper. Emily watched him eagerly, though he wasn't in a hurry, and there was a pause of silence as he silently puffed his pipe.

"Well?" urged Emily.

"Well, me lass," began Ernest, with words which came from deep reflection, "the importance on't is what it means to yeself. It seems, listening to ye, that ye didn't really knoow that these mountains ye had visions of in yer own mind, well that they actually exist- that these wondrous high hills, far better than't moors, are actually there at a place on't Earth. That's part of yer excitement; that what's in yer head has been made real to ye. The other part o' yer glee is seeing a young girl like yeself rebelling successfully agin her world of limitations, - summat which ye 'ave never been able t' dae."

He's reaching for big words here, which sound strange from his lips. But he's right, Maria is a vision to me of how to successfully rebel against limitations.

"Ye 'ave to consider," he went on, "that thoo' it's true fer ye that "the hills are alive wi't sound of music", - as ye love the moors,- what ain't true for Emily is that she has transcended the things which irk and limit her."

"You're so right!" The touch of profound understanding and empathy was enough to cause Emily to pour out to the kind old man all the trouble she suffered and the oppression she felt in her life a home.

Half an hour later, after her tale was finished, full of acute perception and eloquent words, Ernest pronounced: "Mayhap, ye can write to' t Pope, to find a place in a monastery in't mountains, then ye can escape from yer Yorkshire purgatory."

"Don't be daft!" reacted Emily, shifting uncomfortably.

"Ee lass, but I'm not 'appen daft!" He looked at her with a twinkle in his eye.

"If ye don't take bull by't horns, ye'll ne'er get oot of here! Let be for noo, but I knoow some'un" - -

He paused, whilst Emily looked mystified. "Meantime what I say to ye is – Why don't ye try going to't church?"

"Church? What will I find there?" she asked in surprise.

"Nay lass, it's what might find ye."

What a strange man he is to say such things! He seems to see more than I can, all the way round things, yet I trust him - - I feel things aren't going to be the same, something will shift.

CHAPTER 6

Reaching Out

I T WAS NEARLY Christmas time; Emily had just returned from walking on the moors. The landscape was crisp and white with a layer of snow, the sky an azure blue. She had seen a rose still blooming, in one of the gardens en route, though coated in a sparkling frost, and had written a poem about it:

In frost-furred form the ruby-rose sleeps
The white-winged chrysalis of winter's world.

Always she was scribbling, always her mind working, stimulated most by the wildness and fresh air of the moors.

When she came indoors, glowing with freshness, she found her family occupied as usual with trivial pursuits. She gave thanks that she felt elevated above them, that she felt she was a gifted soul, pursuing high and noble thoughts. Yet she also felt so lonely and isolated and yearning.

"There ye'are Emily! Will ye help us with the making of these baubles for the Christmas tree?"

The young girl, glowing with an aura of other-worldly brightness, looked at all the fripperies on the floor, delved into by her cousins, and sighed.

She had been to the local church the previous Sunday, St.Oswald's, named after the Northumbrian king who had in a brave visionary fashion marched all the way down into England's depths, erecting

Christian crosses and burning with zeal to save souls. When she had returned home, before she had time to ponder over the experience, her aunt and uncle had chorused;

"Why dae ye want to go to church Emily? We're nae chuffed, we're telling ye now! Church is a place for christenings, weddings, and the like, - aye and funerals- but why would ye crave to go any other day?"

She had flounced up to her room, saying nothing. And there she thought of the beautiful stained glass window by which she sat. She had been rather aimlessly sitting there, trying to concentrate on the praying and to make sense of it all, when suddenly a shaft of sunlight had fallen on her from the right. She had glanced up to see the light shivered into multicoloured splendour by the stained glass. She had simply gazed at it in awe, whilst the rest of the service had progressed unheeded.

What does it signify? It's mesmerizing. Who are the figures in it? Clearly the man on the right is Jesus, and the woman is kneeling and reaching out to him. I can relate to that; I feel I'm her! It's just so meaningful; it speaks to me of something so deep, so real - -Who is she though?"

For the remainder of the service, Emily was gripped by the scene of the window; even when she closed her eyes it still seemed present to her. At the conclusion of it all, as the last notes of the organ died away, she rose to leave, and realised for the first time how many of the congregation were old ladies wearing their Sunday bonnets. Being among them as they pressed towards the door, she suddenly found the vicar holding out his hand to her. She fumbled to take off her gloves again to grasp his hand. He said his name was David and asked it she would like to come to tea in the vicarage sometime; he had clearly noted that she was a newcomer to his church. She felt encouraged to pipe up with her question:

"I love this stained glass window; can you tell me what it's about?"

"Of course; it's the risen Christ appearing to Mary Magdalene; you know where he says "Do not touch me, I'm not yet ascended - - "

"I'm sorry, I don't know my bible" interrupted Emily, and she had rushed away with her head down, feeling vaguely ashamed.

The following Sunday, Emily felt she couldn't brave the enquiring attention of the Vicar again, so she was lying on her tummy in her bed, reading "Pilgrim's Progress." The bed-covers were spread over her like a tent, and she had a plate of Alpen cereal by her side.

This is a good story! What on earth does "the slough of despond" mean? Maybe it's like that bog I got caught in on the moor. The gist of it seems to be that when Christian reaches the foot of the cross, his burden falls off - - what does that mean? I see from the introduction that Bunyan wrote it from prison – Ugh, how awful! Mind you, if I were locked up, I'd probably write a book.

She sat up, finished her cereal, and reached for the other book placed by her bedside. Stung by her ignorance she had asked her Aunt if she had a bible; and she had been handed a family heirloom, which had a name and date in from 1830. She fingered it now reverently; it was small and black and held together with sellotape, the pages tissue-fine with gold-leaf edges. She opened it, gingerly feeling it was in danger of falling to bits.

"In the beginning was the word, and the word was with God" - - What does that mean? Oh I don't have a clue about this religion-business; I feel so ignorant! I do so wish I had been sent to Sunday-school!

Everyone around her was gleeful on the following Friday, because finally school was out for the Christmas holiday. Yet Emily didn't share the general elated mood, for she came home that teatime feeling real trepidation, as if a fear were churning in her stomach. The "someone" Ernest wanted to introduce into her life was a Sister Madeleine from the local catholic convent. She had demurred about it at first, but he encouraged her with the words;

"Don't be glum; weren't there nuns in't film ye saw, and singing ones at that! Nay, follow yer dreams lass, follow yer dreams!"

So Emily had taken heart when she thought of the Abbess singing "Climb every mountain," and agreed to visit the convent in Yeadon on this special Friday night, her Uncle Arthur having been persuaded by her to provide a lift. She got ready with a mild sense of terror, wearing her most sober clothes, and when she came downstairs was had the abiding sense that her Aunt and Uncle were not best pleased.

Soon they were threading their way through dark country lanes, the headlights illuminating the stark branches and boles of the trees.

"Are ye sure ye want to dae this luv? We can always turn around."

Emily knew she had to press this to completion now. She replied with assent, and her Uncle drove on. When she got there she was abandoned by him on a lonely driveway, and it took courage to ring the bell. A bustling young nun answered, who was clearly not the Sister Madeleine she had come to see, for she declared;

"I'll let you see the chapel, whilst we wait for our Mother to become available; I'm sure she won't be long."

Emily watched warily as the sister genuflected in the chapel, and on seeing her look, hastily explained: "We believe God to be really present in the tabernacle."

The young Emily with a wise head on her shoulders, glancing with disdain at the golden box, replied: "But surely God is everywhere."

The nun looked discomforted, could evidently find no reply, and scuttled out of the chapel door, as at this moment, Sister Madeleine entered and surveyed the scene, with bright, piercing eyes, which sparkled in the light.

I'm dead sure God can't be contained in a box, but I think He's arrived!

CHAPTER 7

Glowing

S HE WAS LED by Sister Madeleine into a small room, with sparse furnishing smelling of polish, and the chairs creaked when they sat on them. This was apparently "the parlour" where the nuns spoke with guests.

"So tell me about yourself Emily, and why you have come to see an elderly nun like myself."

"Well I love the moors," began Emily, "and it was there that I met Ernest, when he rescued me from a bog."

"Ah yes, our common acquaintance, Ernest!" said the sister, her face breaking into a warm smile, "many a long year have I known him!"

Emily noticed all the laughter lines in her face, which were so prominent when she smiled. She felt warmly accepted by this devout woman who spoke a southern accent so foreign to a Yorkshire ear. Her strangely bright eyes seemed to sparkle with genuine love as she fixed her attention on whoever was before her; she had a genuine aura of "presence."

The rather over-awed girl sitting close to her, balanced on an old hard-backed chair, launched into the tale of how Ernest had saved her from the bog that day, in a bid to break the ice. - - "So that's what happened, and I'm not exaggerating!"

"Oh, my dear, how awful for you! And how heroic of Ernest!"

"Yes, I've been to his house lots of times since" - - She deliberately didn't mention the suggestion he had made of trying to find "a monastery in the mountains," so she could run around like Julie Andrews, because it sounded too absurd.

"Tell me about your home life, my dear. Are you happy at home?"

This was like a red flag to a bull for Emily, and her traumatic misery with the family who didn't understand her, and so inhibited her freedom, just spilled out like a torrent. She felt she could trust Sr. Madeleine to comprehend as the warm, sparkling, loving eyes gazed at her. There was silent pause when her emotional tale had run its course, and she looked into those eyes for warm and loving acceptance.

"My dear, I am so sorry to hear you are so unhappy." To her surprise Emily saw tear-drops glistening on the nun's cheeks.

The silent pause was not embarrassing, but one in which she could dwell and be embraced; it was a rich silence which she felt could go on forever. For the first time that she could remember Emily felt loved unconditionally, loved for being the earnest-hearted young woman that she was.

"You have poetry with you? Ernest said you would bring some."

Emily rummaged in her bag for the sheets she had brought with her, nicely written out in italic penmanship, and handed them over. There was a deep silence, as for ten minutes the nun perused the poems in which Emily had expended her deepest soul. Emily simply sat wither hands folded, not at all afraid that her work would fail to be accepted or understood.

Finally Sr. Madeleine looked up and sighed with emotion that came from the heart. She leaned forward and grasped Emily's hands:

"My dear, these are beautiful, sheer beauty! Each poem is like clear, limpid water-pool, so pristine-pure! My dear, you have a real, rare gift!"

Emily was taken aback by the words, and flushed with pleasure. "Thankyou" was all she said, smiling with delight.

The nun leaned forward earnestly: "You know I've travelled far and met many people, but I've never met anyone like you!

Emily blushed; "It's time I was going" she said, realising that her hour was coming to an end.

"I mean it, it's your ardour. You have the makings of a great saint!"

She then felt a little confused, feeling clueless about a "saint's ardour." She decided to reply by telling of her attraction to that stained glass window of the church, where Mary Magdalene kneels at the feet of Christ, reaching out to touch him.

"Mm, that's interesting; you seem to have a capacity for devotion. My dear I'm going to lend you some books to read."

Whilst she left the room for a while, Emily sat in the rich silence, mulling things over. When the nun noiselessly returned Emily stood up, out of courtesy, and the sister placed three well-worn books in her hand:

"Read these, I'm sure you will come to treasure them, so you can keep them. And the same goes for this!" She thrust something cold and metallic into Emily's hands. "Goodbye now, my dear, I'm sure you will come again. God bless you, in the name of the Father, son and spirit." And she made a sign in the air over Emily's forehead.

Emily stumbled out of the convent's door, clutching her gifts, feeling stunned.

I'm so glad my uncle is not coming to collect me, so I can walk through the dark to catch a bus from Yeadon, so I can think and get my head around all this. What happened in there, what happened? What has been done to me? Why do I feel this glow, this warmth in side of me, which I've never ever felt before? It's like something has rushed in and taken my being captive. It's like nothing on earth. What wonderful things she said to me, what wonderful rich silences! And she blessed me, I've never been blessed before! And she seemed to know me, understand me, accept me really deeply, so deeply! She seemed to see me as I am, the very depths and heart of me, and love me! And she cried, she shed tears for my pain! Oh the world will never be the same again! And what is this she gave me?

She opened her left hand which she had thrust in to her pocket, and there gleaming in the lamplight as her feet pursued her way through the dark streets, was a golden-looking crucifix, upon which the figure of a suffering Christ hung limply. Emily didn't know what to do, so she kissed it.

In her bedroom a few days later, Emily was gingerly examining the books she had been given - they were partly stuck with sellotape, so she felt rough handling would make them fall apart. She read the back covers, intrigued; they were all written in medieval times- Imitation of Christ, Revelations of Divine Love, Cloud of Unknowing. The Dame Julian book seemed the most fascinating. Suddenly her Aunt who was cleaning the bedrooms, knocked on the door and thrust her way in;

"Oh Emily ye haven't placed that ugly thing on the wall!"

Her Aunt's dismay was due to the fact that she had hung the crucifix over her bed. Nothing had previously been said about the Zen picture of mountains she had put up, so she thought she might get away with it. She had yesterday prayed by her bedside looking up at it, trying to feel the "devotion" Sr. Madeleine had mentioned.

"Oh Aunt it's a Christian symbol!"

"I'm not having them catholic things my house!" blustered her Aunt.

"It's my bedroom Aunt, and I'll do as I like; please get out of my bedroom!"

She groaned, as her Aunt retreated, and threw herself in dismay on her bed.

I have to get away! I'm not going to settle down in Yorkshire like everyone wants me to! I have to explore the mountains of Austria!! I want to be all I can be!

CHAPTER 8

Deciding

TIME PASSED; THE harsh snowy winter gradually relaxed its hold, and the time of the blossom-trees came and went. Emily knew she had to buckle down to work for her O-levels, as the warmth of the summer visited Yorkshire.

Various things had changed Emily in this time; the peculiar influence upon her of the stalwart Ernest and the perspicacious Sr. Madeleine had continued, until she was much changed. Something of the wild yearning in her had passed because she was growing in a spiritual direction. This was due to her continual meditation on the books the Sister gave her and her meditations on the crucifix in her room, plus the fact that she had been to Bradford with a book-token given her for Christmas, and come back with a huge modern translation of the bible, complete with notes. Poring over all these things in all of her spare time, she had become a young woman with a religious sensibility.

Her Aunt and Uncle had not approved of this of course; when she returned with the bible there were real fireworks. And even worse was their reaction to her decision to attend the Catholic church on Sunday mornings, being invited by Sr.Madeleine to investigate what the Mass was like. They almost threw a fit, making their displeasure known, and subsequently they took to locking the door on Sunday morning and hiding away the key. But Emily became adept at finding this key, and letting herself out; there were only a limited number of places they could hide it. And so as Emily had grown and expanded into a more spiritual plane, her relationship to those she lived among deteriorated.

One bright cool morning, when a refulgent sun was bathing all in a golden glow, Emily set off to walk the seven miles to Pancake Rock on Ilkley Moor; she had agreed to meet Ernest there, for she had something special to tell him. She wanted to communicate the secret she carried in the wild amphitheatre of the moor, rather than by his fireside. The family weren't up yet, so she had a speedy breakfast and disappeared quickly out of the door.

She had poetry in her head as usual as she pursued her way through the village of Hawksworth. She knew the flowers in the gardens were spectacular there, and they did not disappoint. She gazed out wistfully with a clandestine feeling in her heart as the Moors, sleepy in the morning sunlight, broke into full view.

"I am, yet what I am none cares nor knows"- I know it's written by Clare when he is in the lunatic asylum bewailing the loss of his friends, and I do have remarkable friends; I don't feel alone, and yet I do, carrying this secret and not telling it the family I live with.

She rummaged in her bag to get out pen and paper, staring to write a poem about the view in front of her.

What do I say about this blue sky? I need a refrain - - "Blue and bounteous ever, bending over all."

She didn't notice the miles passing under her feet, while she struggled with her poem, until finally she put her pen away, happy with it, just as she was climbing the steep hill, where the springy heather and the ferns lapped around her ankles, up to Pancake Rock.

It wasn't at all long before Ernest appeared. He had pursued the path along the top, so as she was scanning through her completed poem with a sense of pleasure, suddenly there he was, breathing heavily beside her.

"'Ave ye noticed these cup and ring marks in't rock; there's a deal of 'em."

"Oh wow, never seen so many! – I can count twelve rings! Do you know why Stone Age man made them? They must have been very connected to the earth!"

"'appen they were!"

"And why do I feel that I'm not?"

"We've talked on this. It ain't that ye'are not bound to the Yorkshire soil, me lass, but that ye hate all the dirt and the muck of it, them cars and smoke from 't mills. But come on, lass, tell me ye'r news! Ye've met me up 'ere for summ'at!"

"You are right, I long to walk in a nature which is pure, pristine, unsullied. And this is what my news is about. You remember when I told you about the Sound of Music, and you suggested I write to the Pope, to see if I could go there, and I laughed at it as a daft idea - - "

"Aye lass, aye - - Go on with ye're story, ye're fair bursting to tell it."

"Well I finally told Sister Madeleine, and she told me to go ahead, and she drafted the letter and I signed it. And look, I got a reply!"

Ernest had a look on his face which was a mixture of shock and triumph; "Nay lass, let's 'ave a look on't!"

His eyes scanned the page which was sent from "the sacred congregation of the religious" in Rome. His hands then dropped the letter to his knee, as his old eyes scanned the horizon with a visionary gaze.

Emily waited on a pause of her breath, as a silence seemed to descend on the wild-swept moor.

"I told ye, lass, that ye would one day be leaving us."

"And as you see," said Emily eagerly, "there's a piece of paper in it, with the address of a convent in a place called Pertelstein, and it says I can work there at the guesthouse, and earn my keep."

They didn't talk for a while, as they sat in a shared silence on the wild moor, as if soaking in the greenness of the land and blueness of the sky, gazing into the distance with eyes that saw something different and new and surprising.

The silence was broken by Emily, with a worried voice; "But how can I possibly tell my Aunt and Uncle? Will they ever let me go?"

"Ee, by gum lass, But I'll 'ave a word wi' yer Aunt."

"You would? Oh thankyou!"

"There'll be no more Moors fer ye, lass, ye'll be seeing them mountains! That'll be the start of a true adventure!"

They sat on that Rock for a long time, sometime talking eagerly in short bursts, sometimes reflecting on thoughts in their own minds, as time passed and the universe swirled around them, and the moor continued, bathed in the sunlight, steadfast and the same.

By the time they parted, late in the afternoon, having absorbed the purity and silence of the Moor to the full, Emily's eyes shone with joy, courage and exultation, with only a hint of fear and doubt in their depths.

"I shall be incomparably above and beyond you all"- It's what Cathy says in Wuthering Heights – But I'm not looking for my Heathcliffe, I just want to transcend this place where I was born, the soil of Yorkshire, this polluted patch of earth. I will embrace this adventure which has been offered to me, I shall go see my mountains – the mountains I dreamt of before I knew they existed; it is a wide open space, a promise which is offered to me. I just need courage - -

CHAPTER 9

Crying

AN ARGUMENT WAS raging in the Postlethwaite family household, in the small Yorkshire town known for its prestigious woollen mill, in April that year. It had been raging for four hours, and was still doing so. Meanwhile the birds were chirruping their spring song in the garden outside, but no-one was taking any notice of them.

"She can't go, she just can't! We won't let her!" yelled Auntie Bessie in her thick Yorkshire accent.

The violence of her words were aimed at a timid elderly man who was gingerly balancing a cup of Yorkshire tea on his lap. He was trying not to spill it, whilst engaging in the argument.

"Ye can't stop the lass! She's her own person now, and 'appen has made her own decision. I'm begging ye not to try and stop 'er."

"But it's you! - you put the idea into her head,- you and that stupid nun!"

"Nay, but we didn't – it was her own idea, she 'erself was keen to see them mountains she clepped eyes on in't Sound of Music."

"Arthur, don't just sit there, - have a care lest we lose the girl!"

"Nay, Bessie, she' been lost to us for a long while. Ever syn her parents passed on, she' been mooning about writing poetry, walking the moors, and looking at flowers. She was never really ours – never belonged ye could say."

"Oh Arthur, don't argue on his side!" shouted his wife, flashing with anger.

The elderly Ernest put his tea down, which had been cooling for ages, until it was too cool to want to drink. He put it down silently on the nearby table with an air of resignation. Bessie was still glaring at him.

"I've done me best to smooth things o'er wi' ye, because I didn't want the young lass to depart away at odds wi' the family; now I see there is no-o arguing wi' ye, and ye'll never accept the fact. The fact being" - he very slowly continued, "that the lass is going to this strange country clepped Austria, and ye can't really stop her. How do ye mean on stopping 'er, - locking 'er up in't house 'ere?"

"Yes!" yelled Aunt Bessie, "Yes, if that's the only way!" Her emotion was getting the better of her, and she was shaking from head to foot.

Uncle Arthur, who had been sitting for the most part taciturn in the corner, got up and put her arms round her. "Now now, dear, don't' upset ye'self."

"I tell ye now," she yelled one more time, "If that lass goes, we'll never welcome her back; she'll be dead to us, yes, that's reeght, dead to us! And I hope she's hearing this, right now."

Emily was indeed hearing it; she was up in her bedroom, sitting on the edge of her bed, listening to every word, until the vehemence of her Aunt's final pronouncement made her break down into tears. She flung herself on her bed and hugged her pillow, sobbing in a way that sounded as if it would have no end.

My Aunt and Uncle are the only family I have- that they would treat me as dead to them if I go against their wishes and follow my dream! - that she could say I'd dead to them! Oh I can't bear it!

She seemed to cry herself into oblivion, because the next thing she knew, the voices downstairs were quieter. After the crescendo, Ernest seemed to be reasoning with them in a quieter fashion. The hysterical edge had gone from Bessie' voice.

"But how could she possibly have planned it" she wailed, "and found a place to go, and got the tickets?"

"Well she saved up for't train cost from 'er old Saturday job,- she's been saving up for long months. As for't plans of the business, she's been conversing-like with't nuns in Pertlestein, and they've telled 'er what her duties will be. It's all planned – she'll be looked after, I assure ye, and she'll come back to ye, - if ye'll have her back, that is."

Aunt Bessie had been mollified, and as Ernest prepared to leave, she turned and hugged her husband, and declared; "Aye, happen what will be will be. And I suppose Yorkshire and her beloved Moors will still be 'ere when she' s back."

"That's reeght, Mrs Postletwaite, best be philosophical about it. I'll just call up to Emily 'afore I'm away."

Thank goodness, it's all over. I'm so thankful to Ernest for doing that for me. Who would have thought my aunt and uncle would ever be reconciled to that? Looks as though I am going to my Sound of Music country!

She responded "Thanks so much," as Ernest called to her from the bottom of the stairs; "I'm away lass! Good fortune go wi' ye!"

It was a sunny, bright, blue-skied day in May, and Emily was sitting on the Moors for the last time before her impending train-journey. Her exams were over, she'd said farewell to her friends, and now felt a mixture of excitement and trepidation, as she climbed up to this viewpoint listening to Simon and Garfunkle's "Bridge over Troubled Waters" on her transistor. The sentiment of the song made her feel that the Lord Jesus would go before her, and lead and guide her, and protect her, at this momentous cross-roads when an unknown path stretched before her.

My God, the words are spoken directly to me! "Sail along silver girl, sail along by, your dreams are on their way, see how they shine"! Yes my dreams are coming true and shining with promise!

She switched the radio off at the end of the song, and gazed at how the valleys were lapped in mist whilst the surrounding hills soared and marched forever on. She felt once more a master of all she surveyed, and part of the body of the turning earth.

I'm sad to leave you, my Moors, for you are in my blood, and to leave you behind is perhaps to leave myself. But I have to go forward, and it's all planned now.

As she said it, she wished it wasn't planned. A pang at the realisation that she was leaving her beloved Moors suddenly came over her, and took possession, so that she no longer wanted to go. Tears slowly welled in her eyes.

I've always despised this Yorkshire where I have lived- not the land itself and not the moors of course, - but the mills belching smoke, and the drone of the cars on the road, and the black grime upon the virgin snow. - But there's no evidence of that, here, now- there's only the moors rising from the mist, and the call of the wild, and my own beating heart.

She sat there longer, perfectly still, listening and remembering. Pictures fell into her mind of the idyllic time with her own Mum and Dad, the tragic grief, and then the endless arguments with her Aunt and Uncle, - how she never fitted in, and felt a foreign body within the family. It was just sad, it was all so sad, and so different from what might have been. Now the possibility of what will be had filled her mind, had made her dare to hope; that grasping of a hope might transport her to a new world, new relationships to support her, and real mountains to make her lift her head, to dare to climb - -

She suddenly realised she was copiously shedding tears.

Yorkshire, my Yorkshire, root of my being, will I ever see you as Home again? Listen to me, Moors, keep my heart and voice, and bring me back!

CHAPTER 10

Travelling

EMILY WAS STANDING on the station platform in Calais. She looked and felt very lost and vulnerable. She had just been trying to buy a baguette for her breakfast, but they didn't queue, and she couldn't make herself understood, and they ended up all yelling at her. But she had obtained a morsel of bread, and now chewed it gratefully.

Travelling was not at all the fun she had thought it to be; in fact it was unpleasant, stressful and downright dangerous. She had crossed the Channel on the night ferry from Dover, and had found it a true nightmare. At first she thought it romantic, as she stood on deck, with the moon struggling from behind the clouds and lighting up a clear path of silver light across the surging sea. And the noise of the water mesmerized her, as she pondered. *I'm embarking on a real adventure and doing something which is fine and brave!*

However she couldn't stay on the chilly deck all night, and had gone into the cabin to get some sleep. Then the torment of all the lorry-drivers began; they were leering at her and bantering to each other, and almost salivating at the sight of a young virgin like herself, vulnerable on such a trip on her own. She tried to move elsewhere, but they called in others, until they became a mass of brute humanity all goading her and petitioning her in a lewd manner. It was the first time she had been out of the safety of her family in Yorkshire, and the experience was frightening and dreadful to her. Finally she had spoken to a steward and he had found her a spot where he said he would protect her privacy, and finally she snuggled into ball, solitary and miserable, and fell into a fitful sleep.

Now the journey onward, the effort to find the right train which would carry her through Germany, taxed her tired brain. There were endless journeys displayed on the board, but finally she identified the train she believed was hers, and hurried forwards on the platform.

An alarming, crashing noise suddenly halted her! Her suitcase, - the heavy one containing all her books – had thudded to the floor, having fallen off its handle, and then it had burst open! She stopped in her tracks, utterly shocked and dismayed, to see all her books splayed across the concrete, with their pages fluttering in the breeze. A shrill cry of horror escaped from her mouth, as she knelt beside the fluttering pages in complete despair. *This is a nightmare! How can I travel onwards now!*

As she knelt, too shocked to even cry, a porter in uniform suddenly appeared amongst the books, and fortunately he was a kindly soul who did not harbour ill thoughts. "I saw what happened, my dear," he said, though he said it in French, which she struggled to understand. "Do you speak English?" she appealed.

Apparently he didn't speak English, but he knew how to help all the same. He went off, saying she should "Wait a minute," and quickly re-appeared with some rope. Meanwhile everybody just hurried past ignoring her. *How lost I feel on a foreign station with all my possessions strewn around me!*

"Can you fix it?" she anxiously pleaded.

"Yes, I can help. Don't worry, there's time and you won't miss your train."

Twelve hours later she was still on the train as it rattled through Germany, still breathing a sigh of relief, feeling so very grateful to the stranger who had helped her, and occasionally gazing at the patched-up suitcase, hoping it would hold.

I never want a repeat of that experience as long as I live! But then again, it teaches me that even when a catastrophe happens, human nature is basically kind enough for complete strangers to want to help. Yes, I feel so grateful to that man who helped me on my way, even though all the rest were ignoring my plight as they hurried past. I'll never forget it, because it was so extreme!

She was waiting now for coffee to arrive, because it was the very early morning and the strange conductress had promised her coffee and a roll. None came, and she really needed sustenance. *Why is travel so enormously difficult?*

So she sought out the woman by looking along the corridor; she spoke halting English at least. Emily found both the French and German she learnt at school were pathetically useless; she just couldn't pick up what people were saying in a foreign language in real situations. "Where is the coffee?" she managed to ask her in German on finding her.

"I can't give you coffee; there is no hot water," she stammered back.

"But you promised to give me something to eat and drink," said Emily appealingly. She was so hungry and thirsty!

The woman shrugged her shoulders and repeated "There is no hot water."

Emily disliked the woman intensely; *she's lying to me, I can tell.* Her need of food and drink cried out in protest at this conviction that it was a lie. But there was nothing she could do about it; she couldn't get off the train, as it sped its way toward Austria. *I'm a fool, an imbecile; I should have brought food and drink with me!*

She took her seat again. *You don't always meet with kindness, do you?*

She watched the greyness of the dawn, and the quaint German houses as they flashed their way past, feeling sorry for herself.

Finally, much later that day, between the two Austrian villages of Feldbach and Fehring, the train arrived at her destination. She was thrilled with the thought of anticipation as they approached the platform, expecting the nuns to meet her there.

She got off the train, and stood forlornly on the platform, as it passed on its way with a whine; there was no-one there. There was absolutely no-one there.

But they arranged to meet me; that's what we arranged; how can they not be here! How can they do this to me! Emily felt stunned, and betrayed by these nuns she had come to stay with, having come all the way from Yorkshire on her own.

She then sat on a seat, and waited for a good hour, hoping that someone would come for her. But no-one came. *Don't cry; be brave!*

Eventually she went to the station-master and asked where the nuns were, who were supposed to meet her, and lived in a convent nearby called St.Gabriel.

"No they won't come; they're an enclosed order you see."

"Oh" she said, crestfallen. But she was glad he spoke some English, so she asked the way, determined to get there by herself.

"Well it's up that hill, you see." Dismay came over her face; it was a very steep hill with a little dirt track winding up it. He showed the gate that led to the path.

She grasped both suitcases, almost manfully, and started the climb. Every two minutes she had to put them down for a pause, because they were very heavy and she was worried about the one that was secured with rope.

I'll never get there; this path is impossible!

She looked around at the countryside; there were little hills, mostly covered with woods, and pastures, where she could see cows scattered about.

But where's the mountains? I came to see mountains, and there aren't any! I've come all this way, and had a horrible journey, and no-one has come to meet me, and I'm hungry and thirsty and tired, and my arms ache and my legs are like jelly, and I there aren't any mountains! Why did I come? I shouldn't have come, it's been a mistake! How far I am now from my beloved Moors, how far from home!

CHAPTER 11

Settling In

EMILY WAS HANGING upon the trees halfway up a very tall ladder, trying to pick the apricots in the orchard. She had got the gist of it, very rapidly, and was glad the nuns had given her an outside job on this idyllic sunny morning.

Most of her time was spent in the kitchen of the guesthouse, cleaning it, or clearing the tables after the guests had eaten, or stacking the dishwasher. *It is surprising how much work that guesthouse needs; what did they do before I arrived?*

One of the nuns, Sr.Antonia, was very kind to her, almost motherly; the other, Sr.Gregoria, was like a dragon, her bellowing voice always echoing around the guesthouse. But Emily did her best to please or placate both. She was a good worker when she wanted to be, always striving for a kind of perfection. That morning the two nuns, motivated by a sense of fun, had taken a photograph of her by the guesthouse door, and looking at it, she was proud of how she looked, - blue trousers and blue blouse, with a very fetching blue headscarf, which she had taken to wearing to protect her hair from the increasingly hot sun. The surrounding landscape was beautiful, and sun-drenched; she had gradually adapted to the reality of mountains being missing.

Now she was about her favourite tasking of collecting fruit; the redcurrants were easy, but the apricots required more expertise. She looked round at the perfect blue sky, - a different colour than it was in

Yorkshire, and the sun sparkling through the branches of the inviting deep wood.

It's a beautiful place, and so different, and I'm glad to be here, and I'm getting on well! But why do I feel mournful all the time?

She was indeed getting on well, - her German was coming on in leaps and bounds, and she was flourishing in the way she related to others. She was even enjoying the Latin chanting which happened in the chapel. It had taken her out of herself, arriving at this convent perched on a hilltop in the lower foothills between the Alps and Austria's major cities. It had put her life in Yorkshire in perspective, so she could see it for what it was; it had made her grow up.

She reached for another apricot, hanging on an outermost bough. The ladder tipped precariously. "Hilfe, hilfe, help!" she cried, as she half clung to the bough and half to the falling ladder. The nun working nearby dropped her apron full of redcurrants and came running. She steadied the ladder, and helped the stricken girl to the ground. Emily felt so grateful, she nearly hugged her, though knowing it wasn't allowed. She sat there shaking on the ground, whilst the sister wagged her finger:

"You must be careful whilst climbing trees; it is a dangerous business," she said in German.

Gefährlich? That means dangerous, doesn't it? Well I was enjoying it till now!

I don't think I'll want to climb on a ladder ever again!

The kind nun could see how shaken she was, and set her to collecting redcurrants instead. She sat down on a log for a pause. Then she saw huge black ants trailing across the wood; the sister told her they were wood ants.

This is a different world; we don't have anything like these redcurrants or wood ants in Yorkshire! I'll write to my Aunt and tell her about these things.

It was a month later and Emily was trying to enjoy her day off. She had been down to the village, to buy herself a large bar of Swiss milk chocolate, and a bag of nuts and raisins. She had almost scoffed the lot, whilst reading the morally uplifting poetry of Wordsworth. Her own poetry-writing had diminished since residing here, though she couldn't comprehend why. Perhaps it was because she was absorbing new experiences, rather then using poetry as an escapism from a reality she couldn't abide.

Her Aunt had written back to her; Emily had plied her relatives in Yorkshire with letters which described things they couldn't dream of, - from chanting nuns to the collecting of redcurrants and apricots, to the rolling wooded hills and amazing blue skies, to the quaint ways of the Austrian peasants and the strange horned Austrian cows, to things like squirrels and ants in the woods.

She had recounted to the folks back home how she came to her attic room one night, holding the flask of camomile tea that the kind Sr.Antonia had given her, and suddenly a bat whisked past her. She was terrified at first, scared that the creature would entangle itself in her hair, but then realised the creature was more frightened of her than she was of it. And when she got to her room, she discovered a line of those pesky ants trekking across the wall near her bed-head. She couldn't bear them being there, but every time she killed some of them, they would come straight back. Her Aunt had reacted with horror over this tale; she must turn her bed round, and couldn't the sisters give her good old Yorkshire tea? The relationship was improving.

So now it was afternoon on her precious day of freedom, and she determined to go for a walk over the wooded hills, though any Yorkshire person would tell her it was too hot. She took some of the chocolate and nuts that remained, and some precious juice, and went down, through the gate of the orchard, into the wild countryside beyond.

And it was hot, far too hot. She was glad she had her headscarf on, to protect her hair from the beating sun, but then was so sweltering she wanted to take it off.

It's never as hot as this in Yorkshire, but then again you don't see cute little red squirrels like that in Yorkshire!

There were loads of red squirrels, hopping about the grass, or scurrying up the trees. She looked up at the amazing tall pine-trees. The path disappeared into the distance as it wound and threaded its way through them.

Look at this; the branches perfectly meet overhead, as if it's a church. I'll call it my tree-church and come here again. I'd rather come here to pray, to uplift my heart to the God of nature, rather than the chapel of the chanting sisters.

She thought then of the sisters as they had filed out of chapel the other day, wimpled and silent and with their heads bowed, whilst she herself had been looking out of the window pensively. One of them had stopped, and introduced her to another, as "die englishe fraulein," the English girl.

"You look sad," said the other in German, "Hast du heimweh?"

Heimweh, what's heimweh? Emily resolved to look it up in her small dictionary. And when she had done so, it impressed her that it meant "homesick."

Now as she walked in this magnificent old forest, one of the most ancient on earth, she revolved it in her mind: *What does it feel like to be homesick? Am I?*

She walked on for a long way that afternoon, becoming overwhelmingly tired because of the heat. She listened to the chirruping of the birds, the scurrying of the squirrels, in that magnificent ancient wood, then as she emerged into a new valley, where the trees came to an end and she saw a great vista in front of her, - pasture dotted with cows, which echoed with clanging bells, and wooded hills to the horizon, she sat down on a log and pronounced:

It is all very beautiful in its own way, but it's tame! Where is the endless sweep of the moors, the wild loneliness, the elemental bond with the earth? I am indeed homesick, and that's why I'm always sad, - this is not my country, not the land I'm bound to! This could never be my home!

CHAPTER 12

Obeying

THE FULLNESS OF the summer had come to St.Gabriel; anyone who walked from the coolness of the thick cloister walls into the open air, found a wall of oven-like heat hit them, taking the breath away.

Sister Antonia who had taken on herself the chief care of "die englische fraulein" was hurrying towards the guest- house with news for Emily. She found her sweeping the floor of the dining room as she often was, looking all red and hot from stacking the hot crockery from the dish-washer. There she was, muttering the poetry of Wordsworth under her breath again, endeavouring to learn passages off by heart. She shook her head with dismay; clearly the child wasn't happy, and found no pleasure in being absorbed in manual work, and she had told the Mother Abbess so. She had news for her now; that she had been summoned.

Emily stopped in dismay at the news; "Have I done something wrong?" She could think of no other reason the Abbess would want to see her.

"Not at all child!" came the reply, "Just try and be deferential to Mother, as we always are, and remember that we try to be obedient, - it's what our Order is about!"

She took the broom off her and ushered her out. And Emily went off to seek the Abbess's room, feeling both mystified and scared. She had never spoken to the Mother yet, only seeing her as a distant presence in the choir-stalls.

When she did see her, as the door swung open and she heard the words "Herein, come in dear child!" – she immediately was struck with how similar she was to Sister Madeleine - the dear old nun back home with the piercing, loving eyes!

She came and stood in front of her, with her head bowed, - not knowing at all whether she should kneel, like all the other nuns did to their mother superior whom they must obey in every respect. She decided to just stay with her head bowed.

Mother cleared her throat; "It has come to my notice, my dear englische fraulein, that you are not happy here" - - when Emily heard her voice it reminded her of the mellifluous voice of her own mother, before she was tragically taken from her. What was she going to say? - -

"So maybe it's time that we send you home." With a shock it sunk in; *Heim – home! This is horrific- like a sword in the soul!*

"No! No, dear Mother, please don't do that!"

The old woman looked at her with peaceful, loving, grey eyes; she hadn't expected such a violent response.

"But child, you are not happy here; I can perceive that."

"You don't understand Mother, I wasn't happy at home either!"

Renowned for being wise, as well as exemplary in prayerfulness, the Abbess looked at her silently for a while, then went and gazed out of the window. Emily could perceive that she was earnestly engaged in prayer, seeking divine guidance.

"I have an idea, which is perhaps a better alternative, which may just bring you the fulfilment and happiness which you so lack. We are all content here you see,- real happiness is contentment, - but you are lacking something, and I would call it joy in your work. I'm going to send you to another place where we have some sisters, in Stubenberg "- -

"Are there any mountains there? - - " broke in Emily.

The Mother responded with a smile of patience, such as a mother would beam upon her baby; "It is not mountains child, which will make you happy; it is fulfilment with the work of your hands, head, and heart; joy in your work. That is why I am sending you to work with children."

"But Mother I really wanted to see the mountains - -"

"I've just reprieved you from sending you home - - which would you prefer; it's either- or." *I have no choice, though there is a choice!*

Emily looked stricken as she pronounced "Alright, it's the children then."

Mother broke into an indulgent smile; "Trust me, my child, it's for the best!"

The girl looked stunned at the new prospect suddenly put in front of her. The Abbess turned to the work at her desk, setting her capacious mind to the next problem to be solved, and was surprised to look up and see the girl still standing there.

"Shoo, shoo! Off you go, little englische fraulein!"

Emily didn't quite know how she was supposed to exit this august presence, so she bent quickly to the hand on the desk before backing away, and kissed the Abbess's huge and shining ring; "I'll do as you say!"

Once she had got outside the room, and along the cool inner cloisters with the well-tended garden in the middle, she plonked herself down on the steps outside the main door, feeling overwhelmed, - both inwardly by the experience, and outwardly by the stifling heat. She breathed slow and deep, to the limit of her lungs.

I didn't know things like that happened anymore! – that there are people like that,- wise old abbesses like relics from the middle ages, who still have power, and nuns obeying them, and fingers having influence over the wide web of the world! It was as if it happened in a different medium- under the sea, or on a different planet!

I will never ever forget it! And the way she turned from that window, - visionary, as if she had communed with God himself, with that other-worldly look on her face! And how kind she seemed, and wise, even though it felt like a sword! And her voice so like my mother's! And I promised to obey her, to do what she says, like the nuns do, because I trusted that she knew, - she knew what was best!

Only a few days later, and Emily was packing, helped by Sister Antonia. When she had finally sauntered back to the guesthouse, the kind old nun had met her, and looked directly into her face: "Well?"

"I've to go elsewhere, to look after children. Mother seems to believe that it will make me happy looking after children; "joy in my work" she called it."

"The Mother never just believes anything, my dear; she knows! She is closer to God than the rest of us. And I can see you chose to obey her."

"Do you think so? And is it written on my face?" asked Emily.

"It's not a matter of thinking, my dear, but of trust! We trust that if we promise holy obedience under our Abbess, she will know from God what is best for us. In that way, in giving up our own will, and obeying the Abbess set over us, we are yielding ourselves to Christ. You have tasted something of its meaning."

She glanced up from the suitcase to see the mystified look on Emily's face. "Have you not grasped till now what we are about?"

It's so like the Sound of Music! And I never understood it! Of course, that Abbess was similar, - she gazed out of the window, she told Maria to "climb every mountain" as if she knew what was going to happen! She made her do something she didn't want to do, - to go look after the Von Trapp family children! Just like me, - she wouldn't let her stay, she made her go! But I never saw the truth of it when I watched the film, - she knew from God, she had a divine knowing of what was best!

She sat on the bed with glazed eyes: *She said it wasn't the mountains which would make me happy!- - I will trust! Yes I will trust, and go where she sends me!*

CHAPTER 13

Sympathizing

EMILY SAT ON the swing in Stubenberg, eating her breakfast, whilst the morning broke, cool and clean and blue around her.

She was in the courtyard, comprised of fresh green grass and areas of bare earth where the children's play had worn the green away, whilst all the children were contained in the hall consuming their Austrian-style breakfast of farmer's bread with slices of cheese and Wurst. Emily had objected to Wurst so much, the huge and sliced German-style sausage, that she had gone into the kitchen one day to ask the nuns busy working there if they could provide an alternative; and she saw one of them making yoghurt in a huge bowl from the milk of the local cows. She had asked to try some; she was so ravished by the flavour that she felt it was like the ambrosia of the gods!

The kind sister had thereupon filled a large mug with the delicious creamy food, swirled in it a spoonful of their own home-made honey, from the bees they kept, added a spoon, and told Emily to go sit outside on the swing to enjoy it, away from the children. So this was the ritual every consecutive morning now, - she would collect her mug of the freshly-made yoghurt from the kitchen and sit on the swing; this was her breakfast. Always it was the best moment of the day for her, in the early morning, solitary as she slowly stirred in the honey with the spoon, feeling in bliss for a while before the day full of screaming children began.

On this particular blue-skied morning she was ruminating on her lack of success with the children, whilst holding a letter from St.Gabriel's Mother-abbess unopened in her lap. *The children don't seem to like me; I haven't at all found this "joy in work" which the Mother told me about; maybe she was wrong; and I was wrong to trust her.*

Having scraped out the last of the creamy mix with her finger, she tentatively opened the letter, reading it swiftly: "It has been suggested to me that I give you a pointer; all you have to do, my dear child, is smile and be kind. If you do that they will love you; just be kind."

It was very short, *I wonder if the nuns here had told her I wasn't getting on well with the children, or whether it was her own intuition, gleaned from listening to God?* She had a vivid memory of the earnest, spiritual, wise woman, and the day she stood before her in the study from where she ruled the convent.

Why did I feel it like sword piercing my heart when she said to me "you must go home"? I thought I was attached to the moors of my Yorkshire home, but really it was like a prison; I was like a caged bird there. I'm not ready to go back; I don't know whether I will ever want to go back, even though the Moors are there. I remember how I felt when I used to retreat to my room when my Aunt berated me; I felt like a bird that couldn't flap its wings and fly! I felt I couldn't breathe! At least now in Austria I am learning to breathe"- -

The morning which had broken so promisingly had been overtaken by storm clouds scurrying on the wind. In the distance came the ominous rumble of thunder.

"We should get the children indoors," shouted Emily's favourite nun.

They were all playing with a ball in the courtyard, the children exultant, but Emily desultory in going through the motions, her heart not in it.

"Why?" questioned Emily, as a darkness crept over the sky, "I love thunderstorms; it's really fun being out in a thunderstorm."

"You don't understand," the nun shouted back at her, as a strange wind whipped up and all the birds flew croaking and screeching en masse from the woods.

"What's happening?" shouted Emily, alarmed at the strangeness of it all.

Then suddenly, hailstones came tumbling from the darkened sky above. Emily couldn't believe her eyes; they were the size of golf-balls, and they hit the ground so violently that they bounced.

"The children, indoors, now!" shouted the nun in a panic; "They can kill!"

Emily suddenly saw the reality, and rushed around rounding up the children in double speed, shoving then all frantically into the doorways. Then the thunder cracked, and lightning as she had never seen it, whilst the hail flung itself to the ground ever more violently.

The children screamed and screamed, and held their ears shut and buried their heads in their arms. Emily realised they were terrified; even she did not like this storm; it had the violence of a demon unleashed.

"Just be kind"; the mother's words came back to her. Sympathy and empathy for these scared children suddenly welled in her.

"Come here children, come here," she said soothingly. "Look, we are all going to gather together and sing songs. I'm going to teach you a song, from my Yorkshire homeland; would you like that?"

She gathered them all round her knees and feet, in the middle of the room, away from the window where the hailstones where pelting violently as if they would smash the glass. Then in another room a window-pane did smash and there were more screams of panic. But Emily had gathered round her the class she was responsible for, the group of 7-year-olds who slept in the dorm next to her bedroom.

"Look, we are all going to go into my room, and sit on my bed, and sing some songs; would you like that?" She held the hand of the youngest boy Christian, and led them off, and they seemed to scamper after her trustingly.

On her bed there was her old teddy-bear which she had brought from home. The young boy Christian was looking as if stricken with terror, holding her hand tightly, and then clutching at her bear. She felt so sorry for him.

"Here Christian, would you like to have my bear? Shall I give you my bear? He's called Leopold." The little boy smiled wanly as he cuddled it.

"So this is the song," said Emily, convincing herself that she could calm the children down if she could get them singing; "On Ilkley Moor ba'tat, on Ilkley Moor ba'tat" - - She persuaded them to sing the chorus lustily while she belted out the verses. Soon the noise of the storm, of the thunder and hailstones, was drowned out by all the singing.

"But what do the verses mean, Miss Emily?" piped up a pretty young girl called Brigitta.

"Well it tells a story; it says what will happen if you go courting on Ilkley Moor without a hat. You will catch your death of cold, and then we will all come and bury you, and then the worms will come and eat you up - -"

"Yuck!" chorused all the children in disgust, though it wasn't the end of the story. "What happens next Ms Emily?"

"Then the ducks will eat the worms, then we will eat the ducks, and then, that means" - - Emily paused, considering that maybe the end wasn't suitable for children's young minds. She glanced out of the window instead, and changed the subject; "Oh look children, the storm has passed!"

As they all rushed out of the room, yelling their delight, and with bed devoid of the teddy-bear, Emily sat to ponder. *I seem to have suddenly got the knack. They like me! Oh, it's so like the Sound of Music; there was singing in the storm in that too! And her love of children made her flourish.* - -

CHAPTER 14

Self—yielding

THE CHILDREN, OF all ages and sizes, were following Emily in a long line through the wood, threading their way through pine-trees on a narrow path.

"Hi-de-hi!" she shouted.

"Ho-de-ho!" they all replied. *This is like the Pied Piper; I begin to feel they'd follow me anywhere, even off a cliff!*

"Come on Christian; you are always last! Come here to the front with me." He came trailing his new teddy-bear which he was inordinately fond of.

Emily sensed she had given up something in creating an attachment to these children, - not only the teddy-bear, - though she couldn't say what.

"Do you want to sing the dwarves' song?"

They chorused Yes, and spontaneously burst out: "Hi ho, hi ho, it's off to work we go - - "

Turning a bend, Emily came upon a huge rock in the middle of the path, in a little glade surrounded by particularly green and overhanging trees.

"This spot will do nicely. Come on children, catch up, and we'll sit and listen to a story."

"Yes, yes, another story!" Emily had taken to gleaning these from a book of Grimm's "Marchen" she had happened to find in a mouldy pile of books, - though she always missed out the gruesome bits in relating them, - about toes chopped off, or fingers pared to the bone, or eyes pecked out!

"No, Christian, don't climb on that rock; go round it!"

"Yes Miss Emily" he piped up obediently.

I so much prefer having these children calling me "Miss Emily" than the nuns calling me "die englische fraulein!" I don't know how I got this knack with the children; it's just come magically that suddenly I love them and they are so fond of me. I wonder if it can be that the mother Abbess is praying for me, that with her closeness to God she is effecting this miracle.. Or maybe it's that they cling to me because I am so much closer to their age than the stern old nuns, and they sense that I'm still child-like at heart. I don't know, but it really is like magic!

"Today's story is going to be Snow White." She was perched on the rock, with her little listeners sitting round expectantly on logs of fallen trees, which always strewed this old forest.

"Is that the one with the dwarves in?"

"Yes, it's the one with the dwarves in!" she replied smilingly. "Once upon a time there was an ancient kingdom - - "

She looked at the sea of eager upturned faces. *And you are all fond of me as the dwarves were of Snow White. - -*

As she related the story, as close to the original Grimm's tale as she could remember, in competent German, with all the children following the twists of the turns of plot with the entirety of their emotions, she herself was totally absorbed by the wonder of what she was doing, by the combined activity of mind and soul, head and heart.

She breathed deeply of the green woodland air, feeling like a green growing thing herself. *Finally I can expand my lungs and breathe. - -*

That night she was in her room, feeling exhausted by the activities of the day, and yet feeling content, satisfied and calm. The last of the children had finally departed from her room and her attention and embrace, - even Christian who was always last, - and they were all lying in their little row of beds in the dormitory, snuggled in or already asleep. She looked at them affectionately through the grill of her door, - all her little ones! All known, loved, cherished by her! It was like having an immense new family.

She sighed, as she changed into her night-clothes; she felt so immensely happy and fulfilled. She sat on her bed, gazing at the large crucifix by her bed-head, which she had once thought so ugly, but now seemed to possess a wild beauty all of its own. She thought of the mother-abbess again, and what had happened in so short a while to make her so deliciously content.

Oh I see! This is "joy in work"! This is what the Mother was speaking of, telling me I so needed it and I would find it amongst children! She was so completely, divinely right! Yes, I believe God guided her in that, and then she wisely guided me!

She said prayers, gazing at the crucifix, convinced there was a God, knowing her, guiding her, and loving her. She had never felt so happy, content, fulfilled. Then almost whilst still praying, she fell into an oblivious sleep.

She came to awareness very early as the cool morning light filtered through her window, and lay there in a bliss of strange preternatural awareness.

What is this? I feel so close to God, something like the breath of God passing over my body - - Am I awake or am I asleep? I feel as though I'm wrapped in a cocoon of love. And my mind is so lucid. It's as if I can see my whole life from a mountain-top. I must keep still, I want to stay here - -

She was wrapped in this still and silent bliss for some while, until finally she heard noises outside the window and realised that real life was going on out there, that the nuns were stirring. She talked to herself before the great lucidity should pass.

Yes, this is called "joy in work" – "Freude, freude!" She could almost hear the thundering of Beethoven's 9th. *– Being so absorbed that you forget yourself! All I've done really is to let go of myself, and love them. – That is the "magic"! Letting go of self is the magic!*

She could hear more stirrings now, of folk in the early morning, and some of the children in the next room moved and coughed. What time was it? Oh no, this wonderful lucid bliss, like a foretaste if heaven, was going to pass!

All the time in Yorkshire I was striving to be free, to get away from the people and the grime of Yorkshire, from what seemed to limit me, like my life at home, by somehow losing myself in poetry, in moors and mountains, trying to transcend. But finally I have self-transcended by letting go of self, by self-yielding. Is it self-yielding to God or to Love? That's it; I've suddenly self-yielded to God!

Emily lay there, perfectly still, afraid to move lest her vision faded. She dared to think some more, aware that the precious time was coming to an end.

Yes, in letting go of my eager clinging to self, and moors and mountains, I've learned to love children, because somewhere along the line I self-yielded! Why didn't someone tell me about this before? Then she remembered how some of the books Sr. Madeleine had given her had spoken of such a thing. And she remembered the kind, twinkling eyes of the nun, and the wisdom too of the Mother abbess, and knew that the same had happened to them!

This is being able to breathe, this is ultimate freedom! I feel like a bird, finally free and able to fly!

CHAPTER 15

Breathing

A CHANGE HAD COME over Emily, since her lucid experience of that night, which was to be compared with a visitation from God. She was no longer the self-bound girl who had left Yorkshire. Joy and love radiated from her; she was capable and caring with children, and a happiness to be with.

At the moment she was sitting on the steps, washing something with soapy water and scrubbing with a toothbrush. She was soon to leave Stubenberg and wanted to take one precious item with her. Her busy work attracted the little Christian's attention, who wanted to know what she was cleaning.

She lifted it to show him the crucifix from her room, which since the theophany there had come to mean a lot to Emily. When she had asked the nuns if she could take it off the wall, they replied "Of course; we have plenty of crosses." It was very dirty though, rimed with centuries of dust and dirt.

"Mitnehmen?" echoed Christian, "Why do you say you want to take it with you? You are not going anywhere, are you, and leaving me?"

Emily could see he was close to tears and biting his lip to keep them back, so she put her arms round him: "Oh Christian, you have to leave here too! This is a holiday home, it's not open in the winter!"

"Does that mean I have to go back to my family in the town, and go to school?" His tears were shed in earnest now, and her heart brimmed in feeling sorry for him. He pulled at the word "schule" as if it were the saddest word in the world.

"But I'm going to school too Christian! I'm being sent to teach in a school in Krems, - it's on the Danube near Vienna."

The internal workings of the Benedictine order had once again arranged this move for Emily; she never ceased to wonder at the inter-connectedness of the Benedictines; every abbess seemed to know every other. Aunt Bessie had pleaded with her in her letters to come home, - back to her Yorkshire roots, instead of "wandering round a foreign country," but Emily knew what awaited her, - endless talk of her "getting a husband and settling down." So she had defiantly replied - "I'm not ready to come home."

She looked down at the young sobbing boy next to her, wiped her soapy hands, and cuddled him; "Don't take on so, don't be heart-broken. We've both been happy here, but things just have to change and move on. We can't just keep things as they are forever!"

"But don't things always have a happy ending, like Grimm's fairy-stories?"

"I'm afraid they don't in real life; sometimes it seems a happy ending because the story is paused in the middle, but in the end nearly all stories are sad."

I think Shakespeare proves this; I prefer the tragedies to the comedies, because they all end sadly, with death, like real life does. I mustn't say that to this little boy - -

She picked him up and cuddled him, assuming the cross was clean enough.

"And you have something to take with you Christian, to remember this place and me; you have my teddy-bear."

Oh God, that's ominous! I've swapped a teddy-bear for a crucifix!

She carried the child with her as she went to check the security of her suitcase straps. This move wasn't at all like the timid manner in which she had initially arrived and climbed the hill to St.Gabriel; she was going confidently.

More adventures are awaiting me.

Krems was a quaint medieval town, situated by a strategic crossing over the river Danube; its bridge was crucial to the

North-East region of Austria. Its ancient red-roofed buildings were cute and clean-looking as they nestled near the river. It was the Wachau area, known above all for its plenteous apricot trees and hillside vines.

Emily readily settled in there. As it was a school in which she was to teach conversational English to the younger classes, it meant she had to do a crash course in the grammar of her own language, so she could see the equivalence in German. But she went to it with a will, and soon became good at the job they had assigned her. The children flocked around her, and she was lauded and loved by them. So at the young age of 19 she had become a teacher! She had found a vocation, in which she excelled, which gave a meaning to her days, and made her happy.

She didn't find anyone to replace the intense affection of Christian, - the little boy who had become a part of her own soul's history, - though she was popular and liked by the 9-year-olds she taught because of her natural empathy with the young. So she began to fill her spare time with writing poetry again, walking in the pretty Wachau region in her spare time, and the verse she produced had a strength and a joy which it had not possessed before.

So it came to pass, after wintering there, and experiencing a snowy Austrian Christmas, - when one day she had visited Vienna and been impressed by the fine buildings, horses and statues, - she found herself in the very early spring, walking through the woods, with her head down writing in her poetry book.

She had been to see the Drachenfels, the fortress where the medieval English king, Richard II, had been imprisoned and incarcerated, and a ransom demanded. It was a nice romantic story, attractive to Emily, because a lute-player called Blondel had played beneath his window, thus discovering where he was and helping his escape. Emily had happily and trustingly followed the marks on the trees which marked the path, slashes of colour between white bars, which corresponded to colours on the map. She had been reflecting on how her Aunt kept telling her to "come home" – to which she always responded "Not yet."

Austria hasn't finished with me yet. There's something in the soil and the water and the land itself which makes you grow. I feel finally free from my Yorkshire constriction; I've come to know myself, and breathe and flourish.

Her lungs expanded to breathe the air of the forest. *Yes I can breathe, I am myself, and free.*

In her preoccupation, struggling to create a rhyme, - failing to see the next marked tree but turning to realise she couldn't identify the previous one,- she realised she was lost. Alone and lost a wood, she suddenly felt chilled. On her way there she was enchanted by the apricot-blossom, beginning to flower in pink swathes near the river-valley, and all the vines on the slopes, and it had seemed magical. Now suddenly, as she realised she was lost, and coldness and darkness seemed to be descending, the magic faded.

There was a crackling of wood behind her and she turned to see a stranger nearby. She was relieved by his presence in her lostness, - "verirrt" she explained, lost the path. He happened to be a teacher at the same school, so she trusted him, and he led her back to Krems, in the gathering gloom. As they parted he leaned over and, only for a moment, kissed her. He murmured something, which she translated as;

"I love you, in the moment."

That first genuine kiss from a man awakened something in Emily.

"Joy in work" with the children is not sufficient; I yearn for something more, - something to complete and fulfil me.

CHAPTER 16

Fleeing

SINCE THE KISS with the stranger in the wood Emily wanted something more,- something beyond her happiness working with children. She didn't know what it was; it was unidentifiable, but it was always there. It led to a certain dissatisfaction, discontent and yearning.

She had sought to find out the identity of the man who had guided her back to Krems in the semi-darkness. By pointing him out at the school and making enquiries of her housemate Elizabeth she found out his name was Kurt Barenbaum. *Kurt is a nice name; if only he would notice me!* Unfortunately a short time later the same colleague let her know he was married with children. Emily flushed momentarily crimson with embarrassment and pain.

He happened to come across her in town one day in the market, and she approached him gingerly, gathering her daring;

"Do you love me?" she asked in a whisper.

He seemed embarrassed and distraught. "It was only in the moment, you understand, only for that moment; I have a wife and kids" - -

She hurried away feeling crushed, completely overwhelmed by a disappointed sorrow. *It's as if I've tasted a tempting fruit, but chewed it only to find it dissolve into nasty-tasting ashes!*

After that humiliation she tried to pay attention to her work instead, to plunge into it with fresh energy, but she felt discontented, disaffected with the whole endeavour of teaching. Up till now she had been too happy with her own liking of the children to notice much about the way the nuns went about things. She suddenly began to notice how cold and hard-hearted they were; at times they came close to a vicious cruelty.

One day she was in class with Sr.Lobelia; this nun had a bad temper and sharp features, which set off by the black habit made her look almost witch-like. They were going through English work, in which Emily had already schooled the girls in her group, - her favourite of which was an earnest brown-haired girl called Gillian.

"You!" cried out Sr.Lobelia, pointing with her rod at Gillian, "parse the verb in this passage! Come on girl!" she cried out impatiently.

The young girl was trembling, and her knowledge of the previous day clearly forsook her at the sight of the dragon-like features and the cruelty of the flexing rod.

"I - -I can't remember," she wailed pitifully. The rest of the class was hushed with the sense of fear.

"I won't have it! This knowledge needs to be thrashed into you, doesn't it! Right, on your chair!"

She went behind the child and started thrashing the back of her legs. She seemed a merciless tower of wrath.

"Stop it! I know she knows her lessons!" cried out Emily, unable to bear it.

The nun looked up, stunned with surprise, and then began shaking with an even greater wrath as she snarled: "You, you little English girl! Do you dare oppose me! Get out, out of my class!"

Emily fled out of the room, shaken and sobbing.

The next day Emily was handed a note by Elizabeth which came from the mother superior, who seemed a haughty woman whom Emily had not yet met:

"You're in trouble now," she said ruefully.

The note read: "It has come to my attention that you are opposing the sisters in the classroom; this is not your business. Come to my room 3pm tomorrow for a reprimand; it is questionable whether you will be allowed to continue at the school."

Emily went white, all colour drained from her and she felt terribly sick.

So it has come to this; all my joy in working with children has come to this! I so enjoyed it whilst it lasted, but it doesn't seem as though it's going to last and I'll be sent back to Yorkshire in disgrace! And all because I stuck up for a child in my care when she was being beaten! They are clearly going to side with Sr.Lobelia, who won't tell the truth, and no-one will listen to my voice! Oh why did I ever come to Austria! This is the pits!

An alternative idea suddenly leapt into her head; she wouldn't even appear for her reprimand; she would leave! She would leave now, straightaway; she would pack and be off tomorrow morning! *I'm leaving! I don't know where I'm going, I'm just going!*

The next twenty-four hours was a flurry of activity; she went into town and bought a khaki rucksack, and food to put in it; she had already bought good hiking –boots. She cleared up her room, and packed everything she couldn't take carefully in her suitcases. *Am I really going to leave my precious books behind? Well I have to, I can't carry them with me if I'm hiking!*

After a day of industrious preparation, she lay in bed that night vaguely full of doubts. Suddenly the idea of just leaving and setting off with nowhere to go seemed completely ridiculous. The trouble was she had little money, very little money, and what's more she had nowhere to go. And she so resisted the idea of returning to Yorkshire; surely Austria hadn't finished with her yet! *I haven't even seen the high mountains yet, I haven't been to Sound of Music country! Shall I go there, to Salzburg? I have to go though, I just have to go! Am I really going to go, without knowing where I am going?*

It was a concatenation of circumstances which was driving her to this, though she was only dimly aware of them. She was disappointed in love, that's true, so she was left yearning for something, and also disaffected with teaching, having perceived the cold cruelty of some of the sisters. Added to that mix, she also wanted to escape whatever reprimand or doom lay before her; being sent back to Yorkshire would be a doom. It was something of her native rebelliousness which made her take the choice.

I don't know what I'm fleeing from, or what I'm seeking; only that I'm fleeing, and only that I'm seeking. Am I really going to set off tomorrow morning?

The morning came. She embraced Elizabeth, as she entrusted her suitcase to her: *Hold on! my cross, from my room in Stubenberg; I must take it!*

She stuffed the cross precariously into the top of her rucksack. She was ready! She shouldered it and she left, leaving empty space behind her.

But the memory of her closeness to God under that cross, made her decide to go first to the church, the cathedral in the town, to ask for God's guidance or blessing, or something. She knelt in all sincerity but no guiding voice came; the church seemed empty of people and void of God's presence.

But as she left her eye was caught by poster on the notice-board, which read: "Come to Stift Seckau for Easter." Something about the poster attracted her; it seemed radiant with a white, divine light, picturing saintly monks kneeling before an altar. She quickly got out her map; Seckau was 200 miles away; Easter was ten days away. A voice cried within her: *I can do that! This is guidance! Yes, I'll go <u>there</u>!*

CHAPTER 17

Wandering

EMILY HAD STRUCK into the country south of Krems, hiking through Steiermark, aiming for the monastery of Stift Seckau. At first she walked with brisk determination, but then she began to feel tired and her feet a little sore, and the rucksack on her shoulders began to weigh much more and to rub on her neck. But she kept going with a brave kind of gaiety, and she got used to the sensation. She was determined to keep going, with 200 miles in front of her, getting into her stride.

There's a song called "the happy wanderer"; Ernest used to sing it to me as we walked together on Ilkley Moor. "Wandern"in German means to hike. "I love to go a-wandering" - -that's me now! Who would have thought those days when I was walking on the Yorkshire moors with Ernest that I would end up just "wandering" across Austria, on my own with a rucksack like this? Dear Ernest! What would Aunt Bessie say if she saw me doing this? She would think me crazy.

As she got into the rhythm of walking, her thoughts settled down, till they assumed a quiet clarity. She began to see more clearly the landscape around her; the green hills, the craggy cliffs, the distant snowy mountains. At first she had set off on the autobahn, with noisy cars droning past her, but as she progressed into small country roads that led through fields and up hills, the peace of the countryside seemed to enter into her soul. She watched the native animals and birds, heard the cry of them, and a sort of peace descended.

I'm no longer passing through the landscape; rather I am in it, deeply embedded in it and a part of it.

She had made no plans for sleeping; she didn't have a tent with her; she was trusting in God to provide a roof over her head. This was a radical act of trust. But she made it because an old lady whom she had encountered in the church before setting off, kneeling with her arthritic joints on the bare wood in prayer, had whispered to her – "People are very kind in Steiermark; you can trust them to offer you a roof over your head; trust that the Lord will provide." So here she was, trusting, as the first night began to descend.

She happened to come across a church, from which people were spilling out still singing. So she approached a group of older women and blurted out in fine German– "I'm an English girl, walking to Stift Seckau, can anyone offer me a bed for the night?" She had so many offers, that thereafter she wasn't afraid to employ the tactic again. It always seemed to work. Later she found out why; with her dark hair bound back in a blue scarf most of the time, they believed she was one of "the little sisters," a religious order who lived among the poorest people. It wasn't until she got to Stift Seckau that this cause of people's kindness toward her was revealed.

People's reaction to her along the road was various; old people's attitudes were very deferential; they probably also believed she was a monastic. But lorry and van drivers would usually honk their horn, and offer "Do you want a lift?"

Now Emily, warned in Yorkshire about lifts from strangers, sensed the danger of this and preferred to be under her own steam, so she would always answer "No, thankyou; I prefer to walk."

"Why do you want to want to walk?" they replied as if it were an idiotic thing to deny a lift, "Is it out of penance?"

"No, out of joy, - "freude!" Emily replied, at which they drove off mystified, thinking she was a strange young woman.

The same encounter and conversation happened numerous times. Emily always threw back her head; she didn't care, she was determined to walk all the way!

The journey had its trials. At one village she was taken in by the police, who obviously regarded her as a vagrant. They arrested her and put her in a jail-cell, demanding her passport, and taking it off her. They must have made enquiries, and gave her a stiff examination placed on a stool, in which she was challenged to explain what she was about. Emily thought herself that it sounded "loopy" as she caught sight of one of them gesticulating that fact to another. She didn't like the way they treated her, because it was bullying with a sexual content, and felt so relieved when they seemed satisfied she was harmless, returned her passport and let her go on her way.

It took her some time, walking through the grass and listening to the birdsong, before she felt okay again. *So the powers-that-be don't like what I'm doing; maybe because they can't understand such a thing; it sounds crazy to them, they seemed to look at me as if I were an imbecile. Oh please, I appeal to you, world around me, sun, birds and blue sky, wash away that dreadful memory!*

Finally in the early evening of the Thursday before Easter, after she had laboriously climbed a steep hill on a narrow winding track and felt truly exhausted, she stood on the crest to see way down below her in the hushed light a grey chunky building nestled in the valley. She gave a squeal of delight, knowing from the map – *That's it; that's my journey's end!*

She jumped up and down with glee for a moment, then she realised the bells were beginning to toll. *That may mean it will soon be evening mass; I must get down there quickly.*

She began to run and tumble down the narrow path of rough stones and scree; she was keen to get there in time if she could. *Why is it always harder to go down mountains than it is to go up?*

Then a short shower burst from the heavens, which a moment ago was a clear blue. *How can it rain from a clear blue sky?*

She ran down that hillside as the evening gloom deepened, like one last, mad effort, to attain to her destination, until that moment when she positively burst into the cool abbey church, all hot, exhausted and wet. But the church was full, it being Maundy Thursday Mass, and as she made a great clattering at the heavy monastery door, all the villagers turned round to look at her.

At the high altar, over-hung by a huge, hanging crucifix, a larger-than life-size Christ, the monks were passing to and fro amid the waving incense, their chanting rising to the heavens. They too stopped and gazed at her, - a young girl, looking both eager and beautiful, with bright eyes and flowing hair, all hot and wet, bursting with energy into their sanctuary.

I feel I want to die! Please earth, swallow me up!

"Ahem" coughed one of the monks very loudly; "We shall continue the service; young woman take your seat."

Very embarrassed, she meekly went to sit down, her eyes fixed on the tall and gracious monk who had spoken to her.

The service continued, and the deep chanting of the monks echoed round the walls, as they moved and wafted around in their voluminous black cowls in the atmosphere thick with fragrant incense. It was Latin Gregorian chant, but with a splendour of deep monks' voices which she had never experienced before. It took hold of her, it enraptured her, like some deep magic woven in the depth of her soul.

As the worship reached a climax and the host was elevated, it was as if she attained a heavenly bliss of intensity, other-worldly vision. Overawed, she whispered: *I see the body of Christ really present; this is the truth of the Mass!*

CHAPTER 18

Feeling

IN THE EARLY evening there was a gathering for a meal in the monastery's guesthouse, and Emily was among them. "You mean you walked all the way, over 200 miles, over the mountains on your own, with that rucksack on your back?"

The question was asked by an elderly nun. They all looked Emily up and down, - apparently a young slip of a girl, - appraising her differently.

"Yes I did," she affirmed.

"And what's more, every time she was offered a lift, she refused it." The voice boomed from the monk who had just walked in the door, the same handsome man who had told Emily to sit down when she had burst into the church service.

"I know this," he went on, examining her carefully, "because van-drivers who come here with supplies had reported that a peculiar young woman was heading this way. So you see," he said breathing very close to her, wrapped all in black, "we knew you were coming!"

Emily turned painfully red, unsure whether she did so out of embarrassment or his close proximity.

"Eat up, eat up!" he then proclaimed with a flourish of his arm towards the food, "tomorrow is Good Friday, when there shall be meagre fare!"

Then he was gone, and everyone chomped their meal in a merry fashion, except for Emily. *Who is he? Why does he make me feel so intensely and turn red? What is this new feeling?*

She was so quietened that she didn't notice they were querying where she could stay the night, because the guesthouse was full. But suddenly a voice came from a woman in a shaded corner, who until now had watched everything and remained silent; "She can stay with me. - - Emily, are you listening?"

Emily turned to look at her, as a nun joked, "The Professor has spoken!"

"Are you a Professor?" enquired Emily tentatively.

"Back in Canada at the university, I pass as one. Here I'm just Elizabeth, who keeps returning to hear the monastic chant, and so I have my own cottage. Come, if you've finished; you are to come with me, as I've offered you a bed for the night."

Emily recovered her wits, to reply "Oh thankyou, that's kind of you."

"I'm only offering it to you mind, providing you make the bed every morning because I use the room for entertaining guests; it must be kept tidy."

"Yes of course," said Emily meekly.

Well, this is good, I'll be able to speak English with someone. She seems a bit of a battle-axe though, with her sharp-looking face and short black hair. I'll not worry, I'll just trust!

The next day was indeed the fast-day of Good Friday, and all they were given to eat was bread and coffee for breakfast, but it was really nice home-baked farmer's bread. And Emily had slept well on her truckle bed, and carefully tidied the room, to please "the Professor". Now she was walking in a meditative stroll through the part of the cloisters which was allowed to guests. There was a striking statue of Our Lady in a niche, and Emily paused to look at it and consider its beauty.

"So where do you come from?" asked a voice behind her.

She would know that rich mellow voice anywhere; it belonged to that monk, who had caused embarrassment yesterday; and once again, Emily blushed red.

"I come from Yorkshire; the Yorkshire Moors, - in England you know."

The monk was looking puzzled, because she had said "Moors" in English.

"It means hills," she added, "but not like the hills you have in Austria."

She then found herself called upon to describe the Moors of her homeland.

"They definitely don't sound like our mountains. I hear your name is Emily. Mine is Pater Leo; Pater means Father you know, and I'm the guestmaster. Come, we'll shake hands in the English fashion, now that we are properly introduced."

As she shook his hand, Emily painfully coloured up once again.

"What do you think of our statue? It's a very old statue, and quite valuable. Come, before we part, let's say the "Ave Maria" together."

He began "Ave Maria, gratia plena - - " Emily accompanied him thus far, then came to a halt; she didn't know any more!

I'm totally panicking here! I can't remember the words, I don't know the words! I've occasionally heard Sr.Madeleine utter the words at the convent back home, but I didn't really listen or pick it up, or ask her to teach me. Oh No! I like him so much, and now I'm going to look a total fool!

"Gratia plena, gratia plena - -" she kept repeating, like a stuck record unable to get any further. She had gone bright crimson by now, so red that it was painful throughout her body. She had never in her life panicked so deeply.

Fortunately the compassionate eyes of Pater Leo interpreted her difficulty, though he must have thought it strange that a Catholic who turned up at a monastery didn't know the traditional prayer to Our Lady - -Then he twigged it; she wasn't Catholic! He suddenly felt a wave of sympathy for her, was sorry he had put her on the spot, and he too turned red.

"It's okay, I'll say it." And he finished the recitation.

They both walked away from the statue, along the cloister, with an intense feeling; "that was awful!" Emily's face was tear-streaked.

When she could think at all, hours later, she reflected: *Was it really a bad experience though, or did it bind us together with deep empathy; was it actually "full of awe"? I have feelings that I cannot understand.*

That very afternoon Emily was straying through the rich green fields which surrounded the monastery. She had seen a sign which said "Achtung Vieh," but translated it as "beware cows." She didn't perceive any danger in the amicable cows who were dotted around, so now she was meandering among them meditatively.

Then she heard her name called; "Emily, Emily! This way, quick, schnell!"

It was the rich voice of her favourite monk, holding the gate open for her.

She was about to answer "Why, what's wrong?" when she looked up to see a bull pawing the ground and snorting at just a short distance away from her.

"Don't run; back off slowly!" Pater Leo was shouting, "Come this way."

Emily scrambled as fast as she could, and the bull ended up charging at her. She got to the gate which the monk held open for her just in time, with the breath bursting in her body. She collapsed almost into his arms, and he held her briefly, before he pulled away.

"Didn't you see the sign? Is your German not good enough? Oh I see, you probably didn't know Vieh means cattle, with bulls included. I've seen an English person make that mistake before."

He looked down compassionately on the panting Emily: "Are you alright?"

"You saved my life," muttered Emily, collapsed on the grass.

They in-dwellt the moment, looking deeply into each others' eyes. *How strongly I feel, enough to take my breath away, all of myself intense and turbulent!*

CHAPTER 19

Tempting

THERE WAS A strange hush as the guests ate breakfast on Holy Saturday, partly due to the sombreness of the day's story – Christ resting in the tomb.

"I hear you were saved from a bull yesterday!" declared the Professor.

Emily went painfully red at the thought of it, from embarrassment and strong feelings; the Professor seemed to know everything!

Ever since she had met Pater Leo, from the first moment he had spoken when she entered the church, Emily's feelings had been confused, disturbed, scattered in some new way that she had never experienced before. On the grass after the incident with the bull, the moment seemed to last forever as they gazed into each other's eyes until lost there; until finally Pater Leo had held out a hand to help her up and they had parted, with abundant thanks on her part, and a blushing awareness on his. This is what she was remembering now, when the subject was brought up, imparting a flushing glow to her cheeks.

We seem to be dancing around each other with intensity and tenderness. Is this real or am I imagining it? Does he return my feelings?

In the afternoon, as she walked along the paths through the green fields, which were dotted with spring flowers, there he was again! – reclining on the grass amid the flowers, pensively reading a book, just below the edge of the trees. She came upon him suddenly, and blushed with self-awareness again as she recognized him. *This must be chance encounter, but we couldn't meet each other more if it were pre-arranged!*

She approached him slowly, as he seemed absorbed in the book, and gingerly spoke a greeting – "Gruss Gott."

"Oh it's you again Emily! I was just reading the passion story one more time."

And he put down the bible on the grass beside him.

"I just want to say, that there's a lot I feel I don't know,"- she inwardly grimaced as she remembered the incident by the statue, - "I mean about the gospels, Catholicism, and the like," – there was a pause, as she gathered courage, and he gazed at her attentively, - "Will you teach me?"

He smiled, answering slowly and deliberately; "Yes, I might teach you."

He got to his feet and brushed down the grass from his black garment. "Do you know the names of these flowers in German? I could teach you that for starters."

And so they wandered pleasantly around the fields for a time, as shadows of cumulus clouds and patches of sunlight rushed across the landscape, and a soft wind blew around them, and the monk kept stooping and picking flowers to show to Emily and explain their names. "This one is Marguerite " - -

Meanwhile they conversed. "What were you doing at Krems?"

"I've been working with children. I enjoy working with children: I found "joy in my work" as Mother Abbess said I would." She didn't explain how the ideal had gone rather sour at Krems.

"We have no children here." He continued to examine flowers, before adding: "However I'm in charge of the guesthouse, and although we have some regular cleaning help, I know all the windows need cleaning. And there's a lot of windows." - He smiled at the mild joke. - "You could help with that."

"Yes, I could," – a great happiness bounded in Emily – "I'm not afraid of climbing ladders."

"In that case you can stay for a while, - I can find a bit of time for teaching you; and I'm sure there's always jobs we can find for willing hands to do. For a start you can come to the talk tonight, if you like - could you came to the Kaisersaal at 8pm, a while before we start the Easter Vigil?"

"Yes, yes, I will come," she murmured in a daze of sweet happiness.

The monk was still dividing flowers in his hands, explaining their names to her, making her rack her brains: "O yes, that is "harebells," rather the same in English; and that is exactly the same, - "buttercup"- we have lots of those in Yorkshire. Why is it that they've come up with the same names? I suppose the yellow looks buttery! - -"

They were standing very close together, they suddenly found, and she felt his breath as he bent over her, - leaning forward with a tall elegance which reflected complete attentiveness upon her and the flowers in their hands.

She suddenly blushed a painful red, as feelings unbidden rushed through her.

"What's the matter?" he asked innocently.

"Oh it's nothing, nothing." And she moved away from his closeness.

This is "close encounter"; I never been this close to anyone before; I could feel his breath passing over my soul, singing it alive! All of my life I've never been so happy; I've been wrapped self-oblivious in a moment of genuine bliss.

At the next meal-time Elizabeth, - otherwise known as the Professor, for her superior knowing, - looked at her and noticed the doe-like puppy-love in her eyes. Emily realised she saw it, and blushed deeply.

"I need to talk with you," said the older woman ominously.

After the meal she approached Emily in a parlour that was set aside for conversation, and opened in a friendly manner; "I thought I might help you."

The girl was apprehensive; "Help me, how?"

"I want you to write an essay for me on the subject of idealism in Shakespeare; I know you can do it, I suspect you are highly intelligent. If you show promise, we shall see. - -"

"And why exactly? What do you have in mind?"

"Well you don't want to go back to your Yorkshire Moors do you, after all your adventures and experiences?"

Emily looked down and twisted her fingers; No, she didn't!

"And another thing, " – Emily could see something painful coming – "You must put a stop to this liaison with Pater Leo, - I know you probably see it as romantic love, but it threatens everything he has given his life unto. It just doesn't do, Emily, wandering around with monks in fields, picking flowers, getting as close as that! He should have had more sense, but you – you are tempting him!"

Emily went red this time to the very roots of her hair. "How did you know?" she stammered.

"Ah, there's a lot of things I know, and a lot of things I don't. But if I'm to take you under my wing, you must behave better than this."

"But how did you know?" Emily repeated, feeling this formidable woman had eyes everywhere.

"You were seen! And someone reported your apparent closeness to the Lord Abbot. I'm telling you, if you don't stop right now, Pater Leo is threatened with losing his position as guestmaster. Have a care, Emily, that you don't destroy both his life and his immortal soul!"

What am I doing? But these rosy feelings – I love him! Yes I do, I love him!

CHAPTER 20

Enlightening

AS EMILY APPROACHED the Kaisersaal that evening, to hear about "the meaning of Easter," she found her warm rosy feelings cycling around the man who would be speaking. She dreaded encountering the professor again, because she challenged her too much morally. Despite what the older and wiser woman had said, she lived on that eager expectation of coming across this wonderful, gracious man whom she quietly adored. *I live for those moments when our paths cross; is this what it's like to be in love?*

After they had all taken their seats, and she sat come distance from Pater Leo, hoping her intense feelings wouldn't show, the exposition of the "Easter mystery" commenced. She found herself rapt, simply sent to a heavenly realm by the magic of the concept; a man dead, hanging on the cross, and they bury him, and suddenly he is alive, with a glorious new life, and encountering Mary Magdalen as she walks on the flowers of the resurrection garden. Pater Leo was explaining it all so freshly; it entered her understanding in some new way. Then he dug deeply into the mystery of what must have happened that mystical night, - the angels coming down, rocks split, the guards like dead men, - Pater Leo paused and quizzically held up a finger; "But, no-one knows the hour!"

It's as if a thunderclap hits Emily; she intakes breath with a rush and a shock; her eyes widen as she gazes upward, completely rapt. In a real ecstasy she stands outside herself in this moment, which doesn't seem to be in time, - she sees! And light from above streams into her soul!

The moment would be unforgettable to Emily's soul forever; she was in one instant of time enlightened, seeing with fresh eyes. It was a mystical moment when divine light streamed into her; *I saw, I beheld the meaning of Easter – I comprehended that moment when death turned into life!*

Emily knew life wouldn't be the same for her after that moment; what it did was drive her to the bible. She began avidly reading the gospel accounts; even before the high Mass of Easter that night, she drank in the scriptures. And when the Vigil started her enlightened state allowed to drink in all the biblical story, from Adam and Moses - - She was like someone on a new planet exploring it freshly for the first time, even though these Christian truths had always been available to her; but now she was seeing with new, enlightened eyes. That Mass, nearly all sung and lasting three hours, was the high point of her life.

Of course that her beloved Pater Leo had spoken the words which gifted her with such mystical insight, caused even more intense feelings to circle around him. *He is like father and mother to me.* Emily had so been lacking a father and mother, to lead and guide her, to lead her out of childhood into young womanhood; and half her feelings were now centered around this figure who was older and wiser and exercised spiritual fatherhood toward her. More than that, he was a spiritual Master, a wise man who could guide and teach her. *It is like sitting at the feet of a Master, listening to divine inspiration tumbling down from above.* Years ago she felt strongly about the stained glass window of Mary Magdalene clinging to the risen Christ, and here was a living embodiment of that relationship. She had put a halo around the man who could teach her.

Then after the Mass came the Agape, - the festive Easter food, largely wine, bread, ham and eggs, offered to everyone who had attended the Easter triduum. It took place within the monastic confines itself, in the refectory.

Emily piled in to the cloisters with the crowd of people, hoping against hope that she might sit close to Pater Leo. Most people at this stage were bleary-eyed, it being two in the morning and the middle of the night, though all still determined to keep the Easter feast. Not Emily however, - she was preternaturally awake, with all her senses glowing.

When she entered the room where all the tables were gloriously set out with food, and with coloured and painted eggs hanging by bright ribbons from branches and twigs, in time-honoured Austrian fashion, she quickly picked him out and espied a place free next to him. *I can't sit there, it's too close; dare I sit there?*

But she did sit there, for the most part listening reverently to the words he spoke in conversation with the villagers around him; they ate heartily because it seemed a real feast after the long weeks of Lent. Emily knew that he knew, was well aware of her sitting close to him on the bench, but neither of them let anyone else know they were conscious of it. It felt very clandestine.

Suddenly, desiring him to acknowledge her, she picked up a slice of bread and breaking it, offered it to him; "The body of Christ" she said. She immediately realised her mistake.

"No, No, this is only the bread of friendship," he corrected her. In any case their overlapping fingers met on the bread, and she felt the warm touch of his hand, and he turned and beamed her a friendly smile.

But I'm not just a friend am I? Please, God, I need to know if he returns my feelings. They kept glancing at each other rather wistfully, and he must have noticed the way she was looking at him;

"We can't speak of things here, Emily, this is not the right context."

On the Tuesday after that, she saw him approaching her along the corridor near the statue again. They were alone, so she blurted out; "Is this the right context?"

He looked discomforted; "I think it best if we avoid each other for a while."

"Please tell me if you return my feelings," said Emily plaintively.

"Emily, I'm a monk; I've devoted my life to serving God, and one of the things we offer to God is chastity."

Emily's face fell; "Oh please, you mean so much to me; you are like a Father."

"Well we do try and exercise spiritual fatherhood. But to go beyond its bounds would be disastrous, and you are tempting me. It wouldn't just be a rap on the wrist, you know; I stand to lose everything – all that I've lived for." He waved his hand in front of her in a warding gesture; "Please don't challenge me further."

Emily couldn't let go or give up; she sorrowfully appealed with her hands spread wide open, and the words were a plea from her depths;

"But will you go on teaching me?"

There was a painful pause and she held her breath to hear his answer:

"I'll try; I said I would, and I'm a man of my word. That's just the problem."

He left Emily standing there by the statue of Mary, mystified by his last words, as he shook his head and walked off in the opposite direction.

Sweet virgin Mary, if ever I needed your help, I need it now. Please make something work to give us time together, or the chance of a life together. Why does my soul so sorrow and ache? I have my doubts that it won't have a happy ending. But I don't see how I can carry on living without him; he is to me like light and air. - -

Let me just be happy for now, that he says he will continue to teach me.

CHAPTER 21

Letting Go

"YOU REALISE YOU are destroying him!"

The Professor was seated opposite Emily in the parlour, looking grim.

"Destroying him? But I - - I love him."

"And how do you think he feels when you are destroying his task here, his very vocation, and causing conflict in his soul?"

"I'm not, am I?"

"Of course you are Emily; he can't take this mutual attraction, and he's conferred with the Abbot, and been assigned another job."

"You mean he's not guestmaster anymore?" she asked innocently.

"Emily! Your closeness and clandestine talks have been noted, and now he has confessed it in chapter before all the other monks."

"Oh surely not!"

"Are you oblivious to the effect you are having on him? Are you oblivious to all else but yourself and your own feelings? How selfish you are!"

"Oh, I didn't mean him to get hurt through me."

"No, you didn't think! You are totally self-centered!"

Emily went cold; a strange fear gripped her, making her want to run away. It was hard for her to stay there, to hear what else the Professor had to say.

"You wrote a very good essay."

The Professor was laying the manuscript in front of her, written-over with Emily's careful handwriting. "I thought your exposition on the subject of idealism in Shakespeare wonderful, especially how you explain the meaning of Hamlet. You really identify with him, don't you?"

Better this subject than the other; I felt so embarrassed I wanted the earth to swallow me up! She said something about identifying with Hamlet as the misunderstood loner.

"Loner or not, you are highly intelligent, and should go to university."

"But my Aunt says I must get married and settle down."

"Don't you want more for yourself?" There was a pause before she went on briskly: "You have to think of your future Emily; there's no future for you here, with Pater Leo; nor will there be a future for him if you go on like this."

A look of intense pain came over Emily's face again, but her look brightened as the Professor showed an alternative plan:

"I intend giving you a letter of introduction to a university in Scotland, where I have contacts. But before you leave Austria, you must visit Salzburg, and go South of there to see the Dolomites; I know an Abbess in Kloster Saben who might employ you for a little while; I could supply you with a bit of money to get there. Then you can climb the really high mountains."

Emily was overcome; "Yes I do love mountains and that is what I came to Austria to see. - - Why are you being so kind to me?"

"I'm just taking you under my wing a bit, and helping you on your way."

But the anticipation of joy was eclipsed by a look of great sadness in Emily's face; so again the Professor had to address the issue:

"It's really not appropriate for you to fall in love with Pater Leo; you would be the person coming between a monk's soul and his God, and think where it would lead; where would you go in your shame?"

"But I am in love with him."

"Child, we can't always have what have desire! Can't you understand that he has pledged his life to God! I knew it might be difficult to convince you, so I've brought this book with me, which I know you read, - look at this line here!"

It was Dame Julian's "Revelations of divine love" and she indicated a line: "Let go what you are loving, dearest child; mean Me."

Soft tears began coursing down Emily's cheeks, and mournfully she spoke;

"I see it can't have a happy outcome; I didn't think."

Both were affected by the tears, wrapped together in the palpable, sad silence. "Now, now" murmured the Professor, laying the gentlest hand on the heartbroken girl's shoulder.

"Tell me truly, for you didn't answer me the last time; can you really envisage yourself going back to Yorkshire to a life of marital drudgery after all this?" – her hand made a sweeping gesture – "after you have experienced all this Emily, - your soul stirred, enlightened, after all you have seen and felt" – and both knew she included the blossoming of "first love," – after all this has given you wings?"

"No, no I can't!"

"Now that you have got your wings, use them!"

She said this enigmatically before quietly retiring from the room, leaving Emily aching with emotions in the quietness.

What did she mean-"use them"? Oh I have to let it go, this ocean of love inside of me; I must lay it down, not pursue it, though it makes me want to die. But perhaps it is this which has given me the wings. I can sense actually that I have got wings, but what did she mean by "use them"?

A bright and blue-skied morning dawned, and before Emily was due to set off on the train on Monday, the Professor had suggested that she visit the Beichmann family in the village, to get an insight into the poor, common, ordinary life of the Austrian farmer, the harshness of their daily struggle;

"It'll take you out of yourself !"

Hence Emily was now walking down the village street, looking for the right household; "you can go yourself; you're not afraid of a farmer's wife, are you!"

When she knocked on the door, a bustling older woman opened, her old frock covered with a blue faded apron and a headscarf binding her head, from which wispy grey hair strayed;

"Frau Beichmann I believe" said Emily extending her hand, though the woman's hand was caked in flour and pastry.

"Herein, herein! – come in," she said warmly, and Emily immediately noticed the shabbiness of the room. There was an old man in the corner, gnawing on an old crust of farmer's bread, and fatty cold bacon which he was cutting off with a knife; "My husband," she said, coldly nodding at him.

The wife was making topfen-strudel, as a treat for her guest, and the thin pasty was spread all over the kitchen table. But she took a break to talk with her guest and describe the farmer's life, whilst offering a coffee-like brew; "We mostly eat the Bauer-brot I make, supplemented by eggs from the chickens, and sometimes we can afford a bit of bacon; the cows give a deal of trouble; we can't drink our own milk of course, because we need all the money from the market, to help us buy other things."

Aye, it's a hard life!" echoed the old man from the corner.

Emily could see that it was, and felt sorry for them! *This is an arduous life, I can see what hard work it entails, and it's a life of poverty. Yet I've come here, living on dreams; the reality of Austria is a lesson to me!*

CHAPTER 22

Learning

WELCOMED INTO THE heart of the Beichmann home, Emily was out in the orchard playing with the young boy of the family, Walter. Having found out that this was the grandchild, after all their three children had been killed in various farming accidents, Emily felt tragically sad over this state of affairs. Her love of children had immediately surfaced in playing with Walter under the plum trees; he was constantly and adeptly climbing them, whilst they played tig under the boughs which were hanging heavily with their harvest of ripe plums.

Walter was a strange child, obviously traumatized by his parents' death, and when swinging on a bough he reached down to her a small troll-like figure, with wild pink hair, which he insisted that she kept.

Just at that moment the matriarch of the family called from the kitchen that the topfen-strudel was ready. When Emily tasted it, she burst out; "Wow, it's the nicest thing I've ever tasted! It's like the ambrosia of the gods!"

"There aren't any gods around here!" objected the old man in the corner; "just us farmers, living the way we've always lived!"

Hans was at present counting his money, putting Austrian schillings into little piles. "He objects, you know, to the way the church takes money off us at every mass," whispered his wife as if he couldn't hear, "he can't help much with the work any more I'm afraid - arthritis you know- only this last night I had to rouse Walter at midnight, to help me in the byre to birth a calf; I needed to him to tug at a rope around the legs, to get the young one out - - "

Emily was appalled at the idea, and went quiet, struggling to come to terms with the image in her head. *That's awful, this 5-year-old kid trying to tug out a calf with a rope in a byre in the middle of the night, because there's no other help! This is another world, completely alien to the world I know.*

Emily could see it was time to leave, as the valiant wife who carried on the burden of the farm almost single-handedly, looked tired, but she had one piece of parting advice; "Before you leave, you should climb the kreuz-berg, the peak up there where you will have a wide view of the valley and the village below."

She took Emily outside to show her the way to go; "And when you get to the road, go straight across, follow the path by the pines, go right by the stream; when you come to the fence, climb it, and head straight upwards. You will know when you get there, by the cross on the top. Remember to take a stick with you; and don't go tomorrow as a thunderstorm is forecast."

Yes, I will go, before I have to leave the monastery; it's good to see things in perspective. I don't understand about the stick and the thunderstorm though; I'll ignore that part of the advice.

On the morrow and without a stick, Emily climbed to the top of the Kreuzberg, and stood meditatively by the cross on which was written in large rune-like letters: "In diesem zeichen wirst du siegen." *That means "in this sign you will conquer." I think that's to do with that battle won by Emperor Constantine.*

She gazed around at all the surrounding hills, which at this time of year were a lush green, and the far distant mountains, hazy in the distance; *I'm going to see those mountains, very soon now.* She went and sat very close to the edge, where was a beetling drop to the monastery and village, which were nestling idyllically there hundreds of feet below her. *How small the monastery looks, nestled down there! How small are the habitations of men on the cosmic scale of things!*

There was a cow nuzzling at her shoulder. It was persistent, and she turned to say "Shoo!" With a precipitous drop in front of her, stretching right down to the valley far below, the cow behind her became more belligerent.

She turned again to shoo it away. She suddenly went as white as a sheet, and panic threaded through her; *It's not a cow; it has no udder! Oh God almighty preserve me, it's a bull!*

Emily told herself to keep calm. She had been used to seeing horned cows around the place, as all cattle had horns in Austria, and been used to seeing them on mountain pasture or alms, but had never considered them a danger before; until now!

What do I do? Back off slowly; speak soothing words to it - -

It took half an hour of inveigling the bull to move before Emily, scared out of her wits, had got away from it. Then she looked up to see a terrible threatening sky and the dull roar of distant thunder. *Oh no, now a thunderstorm! And I'm not dressed for it; but the weather seemed so fine when I set off!*

She made as hastily as she could to get down off the alm, meanwhile the rain started, and in a little it crashed around her so constantly that it was like walking through a sheet of water. She pulled her anorak around her, but it couldn't cope. And always the rumbling and the flashing in the sky which was getting closer!

On a narrow descending path, she heard a snorting behind her; *Oh no, the bull has got onto the path; I must have left the gate open at the top; it's chasing me!*

Driven to the end of her wits, she hastened on, but felt the combination of bull and thunderstorm were too much for her. *My best option is to face it and to challenge it.* She turned with the bull just ten feet from her, fiercely pointing her finger;

"Geh weg!" she cried in a commanding voice, "Go away!"

The bull stopped in its tracks, bowed its head and meekly obeyed. Even as it did so, a forked lightening bolt struck the mountain-side in front of her! With a sense of relief and terror combined, and the ear-splitting crack of lightening reverberating in her head, she fled.

Drenched to the bone, trembling and white as sheet, Emily arrived back at the monastery. The kind elderly nun bustled around her, trying to succour her, calm and warm her. Bit by bit she related her horrific story. The nun listened compassionately, then with Emily wrapped in a warm blanket, she burst out;

"Couldn't you have more sense, girl! Didn't you know that the reason we take sticks is to chase off the cattle on the mountain pastures? And didn't you know we never climb mountains, or be found outside, with a thunder-storm forecast? Didn't you know that if lightening strikes the ground within a hundred metres it travels along the ground and delivers a shock that stops the heart? That is the way a lot of people in the village have died, including Frau Beichmann's own family! Why didn't you listen to her advice? You are lucky to be alive, child!

"No, No, I didn't know all this, and I should have listened," replied Emily miserably, looking at her cold bare feet.

"What country do you come from, where there's no knowledge of these things?" The nun smiled a look of superior triumph, and Emily felt like a fool!

"Well from the Moors of Yorkshire," she said with a wail, "and we don't have mountain-bulls, or killer-thunderstorms there!"

Austria is a dangerous place, and I'm such a fool! I thought it was all dream- like happiness like in the Sound of Music, Julie Andrews skipping along and singing, but I see that the reality is very, very different! I nearly got killed today! I have a lot of learning to do; doing the learning nearly cost me my life!

CHAPTER 23

Moving On

EMILY WAS STANDING on the station platform, revolving everything in her mind which had happened in Stift Seckau, all her deep emotional involvement with Pater Leo, her overwhelming feelings, her moving talks with the Professor, plus the beauty of the liturgy; and then the harsh reality of life which she perceived in the Beichmann home, and the terrifying experience of the bull and the thunderstorm. But uppermost in her mind was her last conversation with the Professor and her overwhelming embarrassment. She was really being sent away in disgrace from this place which had meant so much to her.

This has happened before; I had a deep talk with the Abbess and had to leave, and now the same with the Professor, and I'm urged to go; and I've trusted they've had a better vision for me. Always the moving on; the lesson is, never cling to things.

There was a movement behind her, which made her soul tingle. She whirled round to find Pater Leo standing there;

"I've come to say goodbye to you Emily."

He was looking immensely sad, and with a sigh he pressed something square and wooden into her hand.

"This is just to let you know that I'll write to you, and all your life I'll be your friend, and honour my promise of trying to teach you."

She held her breath as he gave her a Benedictine kiss of peace, opening her hand to find a small HerzJesubild, - "Just an icon of the divine Master in the heart, you know," he said apologetically, " who will lead and guide you."

She clutched it like a promise to herself, said thankyou to him as she gave a wan smile at this moment when their ways were parting; "I'll treasure it, and my memories of you."

Then she was on the train as it was pulling out of the station; and the gold of the picture shone in the morning-light, as she breathed thankful deep breaths, comforting herself; *There, there! This makes sense in the reality of a journey!*

I have a lifetime's memory stored within to sustain me. If I trust, I'll be okay. Always I'll treasure my time here, but the mountains beckon; that chapter of my life is over, and a new one begins.

In a few hours she was skipping off the train at Salzburg, the sadness put behind her, suddenly in the heights of bliss; *finally, Sound of Music country!* She was going to sleep in a youth hostel for two days, before journeying South into the Dolomites, and Kloster Saben, where the Professor had arranged for her to stay.

I'm not the same Emily as when I arrived in Austria, because then I wouldn't have been brave enough to do this. At the moment I feel able to do anything! And here I am at last, in the very place where Julie Andrews and the children laughed and danced and sang! It doesn't seem real; it's magical!

She gazed at the unreal-looking fastness of high Salzburg, the ancient castle perched on the cliff, with all of the city in its white splendour, a mass of spires and bell-towers, couched at its feet. *That's the first thing to do- climb up there!*

At the foot of the steep path that ascended to the castle was a market, and as she wound her way through it, she saw topfenstudel for sale. She remembered vividly her bliss whilst eating this delicacy at the Beichmann's farmhouse; she bought a piece and grasped it in her hands to take sweet bites as she started the climb.

This is double-bliss; my favourite food and my favourite place- I think I've gone to heaven! Here we have another hill to climb; always the hills in Austria!

Halfway up, still nibbling her pastry, she found a path round to the nonnenberg; *that's the convent where the nuns gathered around the Maria who couldn't abide by its rules- I must go see!* Tentatively she gazed at the darkness of the chapel's interior, peeked in at the forbidding grille behind which the austere nuns still lived their lives. *No wonder Maria was unhappy there! But then Maria found happiness caring for children, and so have I!*

When she got to the top of the climb, she found hordes of tourists speaking all the different languages under the sun, all bustling about with their cameras. She was shown the chilled interior, protected by huge thick walls, and was astonished by the gruesome dungeon. Then she emerged on to the battlements and into the sunny air. She breathed it in, fragrant as it was with the freshness of the surrounding mountains. It was good place to view them. *Look at those mountains, mountains in every direction! I wonder which was the one on which she sang- "The hills are alive with the sound of music, with songs they have sung for a thousand years!"*

In the few days she could spend there, Emily went everywhere, visited everything, viewed every church, admired every Baroque painting, thrilled with the bustle of the streets around her. Salzburg was full of tourists, and she like everyone of them had come to survey the set of a glorious and memorable film.

Emily ran ecstatically along the same paths and roads she had seen in the film, remembering them, treasuring them, sensing she was in her seventh heaven, but a place to which she could never return. *My feet are scarcely touching the ground; it's like a mad, wild dream! It is memories and a dream put into me by a film; but now I've seen it, experienced it, drunk full of its magicality!*

She was at the Schoenberg palace, gazing mesmerized by the wondrous flower-beds, the magical symmetry of the gardens and lulled almost into slumber by the plashing of the high and majestic fountains, when something like the nudging of reality first crossed her mind.

I can't stay here forever, can I? It's not the reality of the world where you must work and earn your keep. This is inspirational; but I have to leave tomorrow. I can't afford to stay longer, as I'm eating up the little money that I have; and that's real! Ah well, always the moving on!

On the morrow she was in the huge Baroque cathedral, the Dom which dominated at the pulsing city's heart. It was a special saint's day, and there was going to be a performance of a sung Mass to celebrate. Salzburg was famous of course for its music and musicians; she had already visited with awe the Geburtshaus of Mozart. She hoped she would have time to hear the performance before catching the train.

To her surprise she found the orchestra and singers arranged around the gallery, high up and grouped in different places, so the performance would have a stereo effect, and she was rapidly enveloped in the beauty and majesty of the music. At first she glanced around at the old women who knelt on the hard wood assiduously praying, looking so indomitable, a contrast to the cruising of the tourists. She had noticed they had all been locked in, by the slamming of the huge doors, and was worried by it; how would she get out for her train? But she quickly became so enraptured by the swelling music that she was oblivious to all else. For a while she was entranced by the ethereal sound, the living intertwining of truth and beauty.

Salzburg is like a wild, inspirational dream; the imagination of it inspired me to come all this way to Austria, to find and discover the reality of the people, the children, the land itself, the reality of myself and of my capabilities. It shall live forever at my heart's core!

CHAPTER 24

Envisioning

EMILY STOOD ON the bridge in Brixen, with the rushing turbulent river below her which originated in the mountain snows, gazing appreciatively at the Dolomites which reared in front of her – orange fingers of rock jutting into the blue sky. Finally she was among the high mountains of Austria, - though it was a region of the Alps which had originally belonged to Italy.

When she had first seen them, - whilst changing trains at Innsbruck, - the sight had taken her breath away and she couldn't believe her eyes. Could anything so majestic actually exist and not be merely the dream she had of mountains whilst still in Yorkshire! Salzburg had been wonderful of course, and she had run around in her seventh heaven; but she had to "move on" as always, to the job the Professor had arranged for her.

The job was supposed to have been in Kloster Saben, and Emily had once again climbed along narrow path to a summit where the monastery was situated, burdened by luggage and counting the stations of the cross as she passed them, only to find at the top no welcome for her. She had proffered the Professor's letter, only to be sent back down with another letter, - suggesting she worked in the nearby children's village, - the sudtiroler kinderdorf.

She had soon re-found her joy in working with children, - the "joy in work" which the Abbess had once kindled in her. The children grew quickly very fond of her, and it was mutual. She found it disconcerting at first that their softened form of German was hard to understand, but then she quickly picked it up. She worked as an "auntie" in one of the houses which had a family of twelve children, and she was so very popular with them. She was not quite so popular with the adults, who frequently reprimanded her, but the children adored her, tugging her hands and begging for readings of Grimm's fairy-tales, as they all danced around her gleefully. *I can see that working with children seems to be my vocation, because I excel at relating to them.*

In Brixen there was a barracks, and the solders often called out to her, winking at each other, - the solitary and pretty young English girl, - as she went often for her walks in her free time. But she ignored them, for she had her fill of "love affairs," satiated by the one true time of "falling in love" for her lifetime, - and with a monk who was "offered to God" and couldn't be hers! *My sorrowing heart is healing in this place, with the joy of my work and the beauty of my surroundings.*

Now here she was on the major bridge over the cold, tumbling river, with only one week left before her visa ran out; and then she would have to return home to that Yorkshire which she had so eagerly left. And she intended spending five of those days up there, - on the alms, the green pastures underneath the spindles of red rock, ten thousand feet high. She had already packed her rucksack, and tomorrow she would set off, - on the hike of a lifetime. *Look at those mountain-peaks, 10,000 feet high, far surpassing any walk over my beloved moors, or any climb ever in my home-country! They are calling out to me, beckoning, the mountains of which I dreamt!*

Emily was struggling through the forest, in what had turned out to be a hot day. She thought she had been following a path; but like many paths through Austrian woods, it had petered out, leaving her mystified. *This is awful; the forest seems endless; now I know why getting lost in the wood in frightening in fairy-tales.* After a time of thrashing through thick branches and layers of pine debris, she made the only decision she could think of; *if I keep climbing upwards, I am bound to come out above the tree-line.*

She struggled wearily through the heat of the day, until after seven hours of hiking her way upwards, she finally did break through from the forest and emerged onto the alm which served as pasture for the cows and sheep. She breathed a long sigh of relief, before climbing further until she reached the small wirtshaus at the top. There she was rewarded by thankfully sipping hot milk with honey and chewing fresh farmer's bread and cheese, - food which seemed as comforting as paradise. And that night she saw the sunset from ten thousand feet high, before she instantly fell wearily and exhausted to sleep.

Bright and early she was up in the morning to explore her new domain. She watched the sunrise brighten the peaks long before it touched the realm of the habitations of people far below. She felt she was in a pristine place all by herself because, apart from the couple who ran the small inn and a multitude of cows and sheep, she was there all by herself. *This is like another world, somewhere on another planet, so devoid of human touch, like an unspoilt Eden.*

So she wandered around, day by day, simply surrounded by the animals, in a deep solitude. She simply watched the rhythm of the days and nights, of sunrise and sunset. Once when returning to her hut in semi-darkness, she suddenly heard what sounded like a human cough quite close to her. She was alarmed and turned on her torch, only to find the green sheep's eyes glaring in the light; *Oh, it's only the sheep!* And they became like constant companions, their bells tinkling as they moved.

Sometimes she would wake in time for the sunrise, to witness the clouds swirling round the valleys below her, with the peaks mystically emerging from them; *Look at that; the mountains look like islands in a surrounding sea! I'm existing in a place above the clouds! My heart aches with the beauty of it all; I am part of the rhythm of sunrise and sunset now!*

One such sunset, her last, as she watched the orange glow creep across the face of the sheer peaks, mulling over her imminent return to Yorkshire, she heard the words of the Professor chiming in her ears: *After all you have experienced, all you have seen and felt, after all this has given you wings - -*

She saw with an inward shaft of light as bright as the sun's rays; *No, I can't settle for Yorkshire after this!* This was the appropriate time, on a mountain-top, to decide where to go from here. *I have to create something meaningful out of my life, after all this has been gifted to me. The moors I loved were only a foretaste, and the Yorkshire I left can never contain me.*

She reflected on the people who had inspired her to reach for more, seeing their faces inwardly. And right there, with glory around her, she made the choice of the path she would tread; *I shall do the exams and try for that Scottish university, as the Professor suggested, and train to be a teacher, and endeavour to inspire the young, - yes, inspire the young!* She nodded, satisfied with her decision; although it would be another mountain to climb, she knew it would bring joy and fulfilment.

As she pulled her coat around her and rose to go down the path, herself bathed in a golden-glow, balanced on a ridge between bright peaks and shadowed valley, she captured her feeling in the song which had once captured her;

> *"Climb every mountain, ford every stream,*
> *Follow every rainbow, until you find your dream!"*

Yes, my dream has been breathed into life; I needed to be on this mountain-top to really envision it. I have clear vision at last of all that I can be; a vocation calls out to me and a path lies before my feet.

CHAPTER 25

Transcending

EMILY WAS BACK among the moors of Yorkshire; her visa had run out, she had left the country, and now her Austrian experience was behind her. Yet it lived in her memory; it was magical, it was intense, it was wild, it was real, - more real it seemed than the Moors now in front of her, or the reality of her Aunt's house.

The arguments had started as soon as she was back. "After all your gallivanting," declared her Aunt, "you have to find a nice boy, get married, set up house nearby, and settle down."

When Emily had suggested she could do otherwise and get an education at university, the answer came from her uncle; "People like us don't go to university; besides, it's young men who get educated and you're a girl!"

Now here she was sitting unhappily on Ilkley Moor, trying to gather her wits and her strength. She looked around her forlorn, for now all of Yorkshire seemed a dreary flatness. *I used to think of these as hills, but now compared to the mountains I've seen, - Yes, they seem completely flat! They do! They seem flat!*

She remembered the day she had fallen on this Moor, when Ernest had helped her, all those years ago. It had set her feet on treading a path, - and now she couldn't go back, to who she was and what she desired, before that path. *No, treading that path has changed me; I'm not the same Emily who left Yorkshire; I have Austrian mountains, Austrian children and people, living in my mind and heart.*

She thought of the Abbess, the Professor, and Pater Leo, who had written to her. She was thrilled when she got the letter, with the Austrian postmark; he had remarked that she should refrain from mentioning to her family that she was in love with him. Yet she knew that love would all her life inspire her, - as the moors had and the mountains had!

A frisson went through her as she pictured in her imagination that moment on the Dolomites, watching the mist swirl in the valleys, when she had glimpsed her "dream," her vision for her life. *Just stick true to it, just be strong! I've been transformed by Austria; I don't need to be conformed to Yorkshire thinking anymore!*

As she climbed down from the huddle of rocks, her mind flitted to a line from "Wuthering Heights," the work of another Emily, trying to struggle free: *"I shall be incomparably above and beyond you all!"*

I'm not "sobbing for joy" to be back on my beloved Moors, like Cathy was;

I know I can't stay; love of the Moors inspired me on my way, but it can't keep me here. I must transcend this place. She knew that, as she descended from the crag to walk down into the town which had lain at her feet.

When she re-entered the house after returning on the bus from Ilkley, she could hear her Aunt and Uncle discussing in the living-room; "Whoever heard of a Yorkshire lass going to university! Nay, she'll come to sticky end, getting ideas above her station!"

Emily burst in and said; "Will you stop talking about me behind my back; it's not fair that you should go nattering on when I'm not here to fight my own corner!"

"We're only saying, lass, that it's not the right thing for a girl to get an education who comes from hereabouts; leave it to them upper-class Oxford toffs! What ye 'ave to do lass, is settle down, find a nice lad" - -

"No, Aunt, don't you understand!" Emily was shouting as she put her foot down – " I have a plan for my life, a dream, and I need an education for it! Do you honestly think that after all my experience in Austria, I can just settle back down here, and carry on where I left off, - or rather, where your plans for me left off!"

Her Aunt moved forward with a warm gesture as if to hug her, but Emily leapt back, to defiantly face them;

"The Professor said that now I have wings, I must use them!"

"Huh wings!" muttered her Aunt, "what wings!"

Her uncle, instead of reacting with scorn, tried to be more probing; "And who is this Professor, and the Abbess you keep talking about, and this Pater Leo?

"Nothing improper happened, did it Emily?"

This touched Emily on a raw nerve and she almost flounced out of the room, saying, "For heaven's sake leave me alone!" She felt that the situation with her only remaining family was worse than before she left.

But then she deliberately turned back, transcending the hurt, and spoke with a measured, calm response; "I'll tell you right now, because I've made the decision; I made it on Ilkley Moor; "I'm going to do that Latin exam, so that I can do the entrance exams and get a scholarship, so I can go that Scottish university which the Professor has told me of. And you are not going to stop me! I'm not going to give up on my dreams!"

"Scotland!" echoed her horrified Aunt, and then she burst into her wail as she saw how determined her niece was; "But that's the back o' beyond; we'll ne'er clep eyes on ye again!"

"All the better," thought Emily to herself, yet rueful for the upset caused.

Her Aunt was now sobbing, held in her husband's arms, who could only castigate; "And after all we've done for ye, all we've done!"

Emily ignored this and now, sensing her mightiness, went on; "The Professor is going to help me with the process; I then intend doing teacher-training. I'm very good with children you know; not that you would know that!"

She was looking rather scornfully at the husband holding his wife collapsed into a self-pitying heap. "We don't want this; why would ye go all that way away and leave us? Ye were born in Yorkshire; I thought ye loved the Moors!"

"I do, you know I do; but it's because I love them, that I must move beyond them." It was a wisdom she had learned from Austria, which she didn't expect her Aunt and Uncle to understand.

She softened with a sense of pity, as she saw the two of them unable to comprehend why, or how, anyone would want to leave behind their roots in the county, the country they belonged to, - to their eyes, a stupidity like trees uprooting themselves and walking about!

"Ye won't have any allies in this, Emily, especially not in me," warned her uncle grimly; "Ye're on your own!"

"No, I won't be; I know I'll have Ernest and Sister Madeleine supporting me, and all the people I met in Austria. I intend to make something of myself."

"Nay lass!" echoed her uncle, as if disbelieving that she could do it.

"You've got to let me go!" asserted Emily, "I do not belong to you!"

With great self-possession, she left the room and climbed the stairs.

I know now that I'm in transit; I can endure my family's silliness, their lack of understanding, and the Yorkshire grime which again irks me, because I know I am only passing through. It's bearable, and do-able, and I have the strength because I'm not the same Emily that I was. I have another mountain in front of me to climb! It's scarey, but I feel equal to the task!

CHAPTER 26

Fulfilling

THE SAME LONE bird began its sweet melody at precisely the same hour in the early morn, penetrating Emily's consciousness, causing her to waken and reflect on the course of things which had brought her to this place and time which now hosted her mind and soul. The journey had started with her falling on Ilkley Moor, had passed through all her Austrian adventures, culminating in the epiphany on the mountain-top, which had urged her on a path.

Often she reviewed the same journey at this early hour, seeing in her mind's eye all the people and faces who had inspired her toward her true vocation, and guided her path; Ernest, Sister Madeleine, the Abbess, the Professor, Pater Leo, all the people and the children she met, - *Which of them guided me more? All of them did! They were all the same gentle hand of teaching, of instruction on the way of life, - which I believe is God's hand.*

She felt so grateful for all those faces, those guiding hands. *With their encouragement I didn't remain contained by the Yorkshire Moors, but reached for the highest. I still love the Moors, but they had to be superseded; I had to painfully prize open my fingers, and let my grip on my homeland pass from me, so I could give myself to new things and a future which beckoned.*

Where was she now? – The Scottish Highlands, in the Spring of '81. When she had first come to Scotland, she had found the university study difficult, but soon she excelled. She flourished at everything she put her hand to, urged on by a vision and an ideal. Now she was that vision fleshed out and made real.

She looked at herself in the mirror now as she was getting dressed. She had blossomed into a beautiful, remarkable and assured young woman, - warm, kind, engaging in conversation, visionary in her thinking.

She was heading this morning to the schoolhouse on her first day of teaching. The governors had allowed to her to settle into the house a while before term began, but the start had finally arrived. They had been convinced of her ability to hold impressionable young minds in her keeping; there was something bright, inspiring and unquenchable about her, as well as a deep and steady wisdom, unusual for her age. Most of this had been nurtured in her by Pater Leo, who wrote constantly, true to his word that he would always be her friend and teach her all he knew. Emily was content with this letter-writing, and engaged in it passionately, asking endless questions which were answered with the age-old holiness of Benedictine thought. Hence everyone perceived that she was wise beyond her years.

As she trudged across the wild moorland, with the cry of the seagulls wheeling above her in the clear Scottish air, for the schoolhouse was situated not far from the surging of the wild Atlantic sea, she sensed that they cried "freedom" and they whispered "home." The landscape in its wild and barren beauty reminded her of the Moors she had left behind.

If I hadn't had the courage to go to Austria, following that wild dream, I would still be stuck on the Moors, hating the grit and dirt of Yorkshire, irked and controlled beyond endurance by a family who couldn't understand me or let me breathe. That was the roots of my being, and then Austria was my halcyon days, - the people who inspired me, and the children, forests and mountains, set me free and led me to walk a path. Here in Scotland I have had the opportunity to grow and flourish and become all I can be. Without those former things I could not have come so far, or transcended, or flourished with my education, or created a new and better self.

Flourishing and creating a new self hadn't been easy, but a hard and upward struggle. She reflected on some of the demanding essays and exams she'd had to face, the general challenge of university life and the teacher training, as even now she strained her legs and lungs to push her up the hill. *Always the hills, and always the moving on; it's what I learnt from Austria! I know I need to thank Austria for creating me who I am; it was my inspiration.*

She surveyed the scene from the hill-top before she was to descend into the valley. All the hills, moors and mountains she had climbed, - they formed an image in her mind of a visionary connection of compass-points, - *All pointing to the ultimate mountain, God's! And all the conversations with people who inspired me; they were like markers on the way to the summit! And what they have been for me, I must be for others, for these young minds entrusted to my care, - mentors, inspirational guides!*

She had flourished by looking beyond herself and her surroundings, being willing to forsake her Moors in the search for something new. She had let herself be led by a vision, a film, a dream, had submitted herself to being guided by others. She had forged her own way by the courage of her spirit, by an enquiring mind and seeking heart. She wondered if she had found what she had desired, as she settled in one place to teach in this faraway and mountainous land. She stood still and cried into the teeth of the wind, - *"have I found my home for the heart?"*

The seagulls wheeled screeching into the wind and she could see the Atlantic glittering in the sunlit distance, but all the answer which came was silence. But she knew with the felt touch of soul-knowledge, that she had forever left behind her Yorkshire moors and her Austrian mountains, though both would always live and breathe in her heart, because this place she could count as "home." She knew she had found the place she was looking for; a place where she could flourish and find fulfilment in a genuinely happy and creative life.

As she hurtled down into the valley, she breathed the fresh air in deep gulping breaths, glad of her freedom, and her dreams coming to fruition. She felt gloriously herself, supremely glad that she had not let herself be bound by the place she was born. She had had the courage to follow her dreams, - to be guided, led, let her character be formed by challenge. *Wonderful things happen to you if you follow your dreams, let yourself be guided, because you find fulfilment. This is the moral of my story; don't be bound by reality, but follow your dreams!*

She was running full-pelt downhill as she approached the schoolhouse which nestled in a hollow. She drew herself up suddenly, remembering the embarrassment of her younger self as she had broken breathless into a Benedictine abbey. Though she was hopefully arriving before the children, she brushed herself down and tried to approach the portal sedately. Glancing back at the whole of her own journey which she had travelled to this place, she concentrated her mind to reflect deeply as a guide to her future path in this moment, now, in this new beginning among these children:

The only thing that matters is the inspiring of others on their path; yes, all that matters is the inspiration!

And as she placed her hand on the yielding door-handle and pushed it a little open, she strongly and gaily heard in her spirit the words of a certain song; *"climb every mountain, ford every stream"* - -

A new chapter and fresh challenge, another mountain to climb!

Further Adventures of Emily

A Portrait of a Young Life

PART 1

Scotland

ONE

SHE OPENED THE schoolroom door.

"Where are the children?"

She asked this of a soldier, dressed in highland garb, sitting on a desk.

"Who is this pretty girl who has just entered the room?"

"My name is Emily."

She tried to insert some note of authority in saying her name, but considering he was a soldier, and an impressively-sized man, it echoed hollowly.

"And am I addressing the schoolmistress?"

"Yes," she replied timidly.

He stood and made a sweeping gracious bow, with a beaming smile which illumined his handsome face.

Oh gosh, who is <u>he</u>? I never expected to meet a handsome man like him today, or any other day for that matter!

She suddenly blushed a deep crimson. He apparently noticed it, but was gracious in giving it no attention.

"Ye may wonder what I'm doing here."

You can say that again!

"Well yes, I was rather curious."

"Curiosity killed the cat!" said he, laughing pleasantly.

"Well I'm finding this a bit like Alice in Wonderland, - curiouser and curiouser, you know!"

He explained that he was sent with a message for the schoolmistress, explaining why the school was closed today, and he came from the barracks just down the road. He had volunteered to deliver the note personally into her hand. He gave it to her, watching her face with interest as she perused it, obviously finding her attractive, intriguing.

"Now that task is done," he said, suddenly sitting on a bench and pulling her beside him, "Come now, tell me all about yourself!"

And so, rather thoughtlessly, she started to recount the beginning of her story: "Well I'm from Yorkshire, - near Ilkley Moor, you know! I presume you have heard of the Moors?"

And now I shall tell all my tale, -"Emily's story"- of all my adventures in Austria; I feel I want him to understand all about me!

She suddenly halted herself. –

"No, I shall not tell all of my story, I'll wait till we better know and understand each other, - which I hope we shall."

She looked up expectantly at him. It was a glance of trust and hope; and he responded gladly to it;

"Yes, let us gradually get to know all about each other, - we need to do it gradually, don't ye think? And we have time. . ."

I'm very glad he said that!

She smiled a warm inviting smile. He grinned with what seemed genuine happiness.

Maybe I haven't finished "my story," but further adventures lie ahead of me! Hopefully! I do so hope!

TWO

"Calm down children, calm down!"

All of them were clamouring with a great din, and one of them was bawling at the top of her tiny three-year-old voice.

"Morag, what is the matter Morag? Why are you taking on so?"

"Hamish took my ruler, Miss."

"For heaven's sake! Hamish, give me the ruler."

She took it from him and tenderly placed it in the little girl's hand.

"Now be quiet will you?"

Suddenly there was a shout, with older boys pointing at the door.

"What is it now?" And she turned.

There stood a soldier tall and strong, looking like a Samson, standing meekly with his cap in his hand.

"He's come to call on you Miss!" said one of the older boys at the back, as if he were very knowledgeable about these things!

The soldier spoke up, his eyes anchoring hungrily on the pretty school-mistress, tremulously standing in front of everyone;

"I've come to enquire of ye; would ye like to accompany me to church this Sunday morning coming?"

She blushed scarlet, surprised by the sense of blood coursing through her.

"And here's a token of my esteem" he added, producing a bunch of sweet roses which he had held behind his back.

"Go on, Miss, go on!" chorused the older boys from the back of the class.

I feel weak at the knees; I can't understand the intense and sweet feeling that surges through me in this strange and singular moment.

"I . . I, er . .well . .Yes! Yes, I will, I would be glad to go with you."

And she took the flowers from him, and made a little curtsey.

He made a deep bow, flashing deep and meaningful eyes at her from his handsome, smiling face.

This moment seems to be lasting an eternity - - How can we go on from this painful intensity!

But it passed. The next moment, looking up from her curtsey, she saw he was gone; the air where he had been then closed upon the blushing secrecy, and the world returned to its normality.

Echoes of fighting and bawling children filled the classroom.

"Do be quiet!"

THREE

They walked out through the woods, when that Sunday came, one of the wild Scottish woods which nestled in the hollows of that district. She looked up and marvelled at the beauty of the branches of all the different trees, both deciduous and coniferous, for the man walking beside her was making all her senses come alive.

"Look, a red squirrel!" declared Ewan, "Did ye see, did ye see it?"

"Yes, look there it is," replied Emily with excitement, just before the little creature totally disappeared from view.

They began to chat about the weather, which was fine though a little damp, and about their work, and how they liked it here, as finally the sun struggled to illuminate the scene.

"Look how the sun makes everything sparkle; it is beautiful here. Thank you for inviting me to come!"

"Aye, we have chosen a very fine day for February! Now are ye going to open up and tell me more about yeself?"

And she put her arm in his.

And walks continued from that day for many days, usually in the woods and on Sundays. She gradually communicated with him how she could no longer abide Yorkshire, except for her lovely wild and open Moors, and how she fled to Austria in imitation of "the Sound of Music," and how she had found meaning and solace in the mountains and monasteries there, and had discovered her love for children and vocation to teach. He told her with equal frankness about his growing up down South and why he had enlisted as a soldier.

Their understanding of each other grew, but she noticed that whenever she drew near, hoping for a kiss, he would always instinctually draw back or flinch away. And she couldn't comprehend it.

The question is, what is wrong? Why don't you please kiss me?!

One day in the brightness of the Spring, when they were surrounded by daffodils tossing their heads in the breeze, she used the opportunity of being close to him, pressing herself against him, to approach her lips to his, just hoping and yearning for that one kiss.

When it came, she closed her eyes in romantic ecstasy.

That is sweet; I can sense all of my body to the tips of my hair. Give me that sweetness again!

"I have a wife."

It felt like a body-blow.

He chooses now to tell me?!

"Do you have children?"

Why did I ask such a completely inconsequential question?

"So that makes a difference does it?"

"No . . I, I . .You don't have to explain!"

"No, I don't have any bairns, and our marriage is not a particularly fulfilling and happy one!"

"It's okay, you don't have to explain!"

Emily's emotions over him had taken an immediate volte-face.

The question to myself is changed; - - If he is married, can this be right?

They brushed through the thickets of trees; daffodils seem to have been replaced by thorn-bushes! She was pulling leaves from branches and tearing them to bits with her hands.

"I don't see. . ." he began.

"Do you have to. . ." she said at the same time.

They looked at each other, and then walked on, companionable in the silence.

She started opening her palm and scattering the torn-up leaves on the forest floor. He started plucking leaves too.

The silence is lasting an age, as we go along this path.

"Of course, what we could do. . ."

"Oh Ewan, there are no solutions!"

FOUR

They were walking through fresh green fields beside a little loch, which sparkled in the sunlight of Summer.

"Emily, I've been meaning to ask. . ."

"Ewan, I want you to know. . ."

Both spoke and turned to each other at the same time, as they often did, so close was their natural connection.

"I wondered if. . ." they both said, echoing each other.

"Go on, Ewan, you speak first."

"No, you, my dear Emily; the lady should go first in everything."

"Oh you so are so gallant Ewan; my noble, valiant Ewan! I wanted you to know I've not loved anyone before you - - Well there was this monk in Austria, - - but you could count that as girlish infatuation."

"Really? - A monk?!"

This is a bit embarrassing!

"Can we skip that bit please; it meant nothing, - at least, nothing between you and me. I love you wholly Ewan, with the fullness of my aching soul."

"I yearn too Emily; I yearn to have you all to myself . . . You will be so glad to hear this, Emily, but I have in my pocket the divorce papers and now I'm free of my former wife. I swung it; I swung it so I can be free to have you. . ."

I am surprised, taken aback; I didn't expect this!

There was a pause, a silence, in which they could hear skylarks twittering overhead, and tiny creatures making plopping noises in the water.

"It's come to this I suppose," said Ewan suddenly, "Emily you've caught me, hook, line and sinker; ye've noosed me by your grace and beauty!"

He fumbled for something in his pocket, and presented it to her; "I'm yours, if ye'll have me!"

As her eyes focused on the ring, dazzling in the light, she first blushed, and then reached out to him, where he was fallen to one knee.

"My answer is Yes; I love you Ewan, I'll give you my all!"

But she didn't say it; she fell on the grass beside him, covering his face with kisses, then caressed his head between her breasts.

He finally raised his head, feeling smothered by her generous affection.

Then he laughed with delight, and she laughed all the more, and they held each other and swayed and tumbled in lush grass.

"Now you are mine, and I am yours," whispered Ewan in fierce delight.

"Yes, now I am yours and you are mine," she echoed.

And they seemed to laugh and tumble endlessly, until they suddenly stopped, and first tenderly and then ravenously, began to kiss.

He put his hand up her thigh and she stripped off his shirt.

I am thirsty to attain all of him that I can. We are to all intents and purposes married, we are joined; I just want to give all of myself to him!

"Take my all," she whispered, "Go on!"

He was burning for her, and she longed for him; the circumstances were right, and they were pledged to each other, and each yearned for consummation; all it took was a surrender to their passion.

And right there, in a meadow beside the lapping loch with the gentle noises of nature surrounding them, he let her self-yield . . .

FIVE

She was studying, preparing teaching material, when Ewan broke into the room, slamming the door open in a state of excitement. They had been married for months now and had settled into a quiet way of working around each other, but suddenly something energized him. She looked up and beheld his face transformed with a sort of radiance.

"Oh what is it? What can be the matter?"

"We're at war!"

"At war Ewan? But we can't be – there's no-one to fight against, no Hitler. ."

"It's to regain the Falklands."

"What's that Ewan? I don't even know where it is!"

He poured out his tale, to which she listened, half-bemused and half shocked.

"Don't you see? Hurray, we are going off to fight!"

"But Ewan, war isn't glorious like that! I know I married a soldier, but. ."

"But what, but what!" He shook her violently; she wrenched herself free and stood against the wall.

You are frightening me! I've never seen this side of you before!

"I've never seen you like" - - she began, and he intuited the rest.

"Aye, and I'm getting tired of the way ye do see me, - I'm not your poodle, I'm a fighting man!"

She felt agonized; "Don't say that Ewan, don't say that! I've never tried to domesticate you, or tame your wild spirit."

"Aye, ye have!" he shouted with ferocity, tossing his head back; "As God be my witness. . ."

She felt genuinely frightened of him, of what he would say next, but he stormed out, kicking the furniture as he went.

And for the first time in this relationship, she cried.

"What's that letter, who is it from?"

"It's just from my friend Pater Leo, the monk I told you about in Austria."

"Give it me!"

"No Ewan, no! It's private, between my soul and his."

"Ye will give it me!" he commanded, snatching it.

She was in her study again, the place of her retreat when she wanted to be alone. He scanned the writing and threw it down in disgust; for he didn't understand German. She picked it up with tenderness from where it lay on the floor.

"I'll not have ye keeping secrets from me! This is lovers' language, is it not?"

"No Ewan," said she soothingly, "we talk about spiritual things."

"Spiritual things, my arse!"

She flinched at the sudden coarseness and under his rising wrath.

"Ye are not to have secrets from me, do ye hear! I am your husband, and I own you, and everything about ye!"

I have to speak and put my foot down; I own my own soul!

"No Ewan, No! I have my own soul-life; you can't pry into that, or take it away from me, - whether I be your wife or no!"

"I own you!" he yelled, shaking her now.

For the first time ever, she feared him.

She ran to the door, deftly slipped through, and shuttered him out.

SIX

Things with her husband developed from bad to worse, when he went away and came back again. He left with a new bitter energy which seemed aimed at her; he went and fought his war, and came back in midsummer like a tower of wrath, his energy beating upon her as its only focal-point.

One night, when she turned from him, he grabbed her by force and yelled; "You will have sex when I want ye to have it."

"No Ewan, no; you need my free choice in the matter."

He yelled the same thing again, like an automaton or a brute.

"No, Ewan, stop it; I may be your wife, but you can't rape me."

But he got on top of her and forced her, though she tried to fight him, and she ended up shaken and bruised.

She lay there silent and impassive for what seemed a long while, listening to the outside noises in the quiet of the night.

Why is he so changed? I must think of leaving him.

When he was safely asleep and she could be certain of his rhythmical breathing, she climbed over him, gathered a handful of blankets, and went to sit in her favourite room, - her study. She wished she could lock the door.

He can't touch me now, surely; this is my own room.

She sat drowsily, feeling distraught and exhausted.

On a sudden the door was flung open.

"Hiding away from me, are ye?!"

"Oh Ewan, please leave me alone; let me sleep!"

"I'll let ye sleep when ye explain to me that letter; ye're conducting illicit love-affairs under my very nose!"

"That is innocent; he is my friend."

"Friend, my arse, when it has to be written in a secret language!"

"Please, let me sleep; I assure you, I'm true to you."

"Ye're whore, a cheap whore! Any man can have you! And how many men did have you before ye came to my bed!"

"Oh Ewan, you know full well, there hasn't been anybody else! And I'm not a whore, I'm your wife, your beloved wife!"

"Nay, ye were used goods when ye came to my bed!"

"There's only ever been you, Ewan; I was a virgin, you know that!"
"It's a thing I canna ken!" yelled Ewan, grabbing her arm fiercely.
"You are hurting me Ewan!"
"Yeah, and I'll hurt ye worse!"

He wrestled with her and manhandled her, compelling her to his will. Something in her was screaming;

Please stop, and leave me alone, and let me sleep!

But sleep was denied her that night, as he so berated and insulted her; she sobbed hysterically until the morning-light crept through the curtains.

Weeks later, exhausted by emotion and depleted by lack of sleep, she found she couldn't quite muster the energy to tell friends or anyone at all - "My husband is abusing me." One thought only occupied her mind;

My husband has turned violent; I must get away from him! For the sake of my soul-life, to save myself, I must reach for freedom, I must get away! I can never be myself again, until I do get away!

She thought of that bright, young, sweet life she had in Austria, when she had left her Yorkshire Moors to have adventures there as a young girl;

Oh, it seems so far away now! I was full of aspirations and dreams, so young and so very innocent!

She reflected on that whirlwind romance with Ewan; saw it was her mistake to marry him, without knowing him better. She had been led a merry dance down this path, having married all the show, and not the real man beneath. She remembered the saying; "Marry in haste, repent at leisure." But she had been so eager for experience!

Now I feel cheap and dirty; as if Ewan has taken all my essence of purity and girlhood, used me, and thrown me aside like a dirty old rag!

SEVEN

It was the morning of New Years day, and snow lay thick and crisp on the ground. Emily sneaked out of the front door very early in the morning, clutching a little bag of what she thought were necessities, - the rest of her things she had deposited in her suitcase in a locker at the station, and this is where she headed now. She had chosen this of all days to get away from Ewan, because it represented to her "a new beginning."

Two days ago was the last straw for her in his mounting violence. She had heard him come in, cowering as she was in her study again, trying to snatch some sleep, as she was so deprived of it. She knew this was how the tortured get worn down, – by sleep-deprivation. She felt thoroughly tortured, and no love of Ewan seemed to remain in her, after such a constant barrage of shouting, insults, violence.

She heard the clink of a bottle, and knew what trouble it spelt; he'd been drinking. He was always worst with the "demon drink" in him.

He thumped on her door: "Let me in, you bitch!"

"It's not locked," she replied, genuinely frightened.

He kicked it open, and threw himself on her without remorse.

"Let me go Ewan." She struggled free and leapt against the wall.

"So ye'll not let me make love to me wife, - my wife!" he emphasized.

And he threw his bottle at her face with all his force.

It shattered on the wall behind her. She put her hand up to her face, and there was blood on her fingers. She sat benumbed.

He could have killed me! Now I know I have to get away; here and now I make the definite decision! But I know he will not readily let me go; he will hunt for me, he will come after me like the wild animal he is! How ever could I have imagined I loved such a man!

When she had stumbled to the bathroom, leaving Ewan in a drunken stupor, she doctored herself ruefully, where the shattered glass had caused cuts in her ear. Even down her neck she found a gooey mixture of broken glass and blood. She sat down, trembling and badly shaken, as if feeling a world-sorrow on her shoulders;

I have to go now; yes, I will go quickly and quietly, without his knowing! This is the end for me! I have to find a new beginning!

Hence she was out in the snow of the early morning, tramping through it feeling crushed and apprehensive, not even knowing where she was going.

PART 2

Italy

ONE

S HE STOOD ON a little bridge spanning a river whose waters churned an ice-blue, running with a rush from the surrounding mountains.

This part of Italy reminds me of Austria, but gone forever is the intense happiness I knew there. I feel small, helpless; I feel worthless.

"Bella, Bella!" – came a voice behind her, and she turned to see an Italian soldier leaning nonchalantly against a buttress. "Bella!" he repeated, with an extravagant gesture of kissing his fingers.

I can understand thus much Italian; he means I look beautiful.

She must have turned a distracted, distraught face towards him, for he said with real concern;

"You weren't thinking of jumping in were you? You are the English girl, - Yes?"

There was a pregnant pause. She turned back to gaze into the blue and white-frothed water, realising her thoughts had been close to suicidal;

"I don't want to be alive" is close to the statement "I wish I were dead." And I most certainly feel I have nothing to live for.

She gazed down again, and the wildness of the water entranced her. But suddenly his arm held her at the elbow;

"You don't want to throw your life away - - a pretty young thing like you! Why, you are. . .how do you say? . .beautiful!"

I don't feel beautiful" she said with a leaden voice and dull eyes.

"But you are, my darling! Look, let me spend some time with you and show you a good time; I'll soon cheer you."

She remained unresponsive.

"Look, I have my furlough coming up, - that's two weeks when I can show you the sights of my beloved Italy. She's a beautiful country, as you are beautiful. You belong together."

He was now winning his way a little into her-closed down brain and heart.

"If you really think so, if you think I could. . ."

"Yes you can, my darling! You can cheer up and come back to life. I don't know what has happened to you, to make you so down, but I'll soon have you right as rain again. Trust me!"

"Trust you? I feel at the moment it is a bad idea to trust any man, - they are full of deceit and empty promises."

"Oh my darling!"- he put his hand on his chest as if personally offended, - "you mustn't say that! I don't know what has happened to you; it must have been something very bad."

"Yes, it was very bad, - horrendous!"

"Don't lose heart, my little English darling!"

I wonder how often he's going to call me his "little English darling"! His intentions seem good at any rate. He seems genuine and kind. It might heal my hurt heart and do me good . . .

She smiled on him at the thought. He smiled back, and they felt they had made a connection. And she smiled at him because, in this foreign place where she felt a stranger, it felt she had made a friend.

And they walked off together, away from the danger of the bridge and its tempting waters.

TWO

The first thing she said to him when they saw each other the next day, - for they had agreed to meet on the bridge - was;

"How did you know I was English?"

He explained how one of his fellow-soldiers had seen her in the café trying to order in Italian, and they had shared laughter over it, and he was told to look out for her pretty blue flowery dress, distinctive among Italian fabrics. "She looked English" he had said.

Well at least I'm known as English, and a Yorkshire lass, - far better than being Scottish!

She involuntarily shuddered at the thought of the brutality she had recently suffered in the land of the Scots.

I never my whole life long want to go back to that dreadful place. But I'm willing for a while at least to embrace what Italy has to offer. If I can just heal, I may regain my ability to return home to the Moors . . .

She reached out a hand to take his; "I don't know your name."

"I don't know yours, but I can guess it will be a pretty English name."

Gino,- for that was the handsome soldier's name, - from that day on spent a lot of his spare time climbing in the foothills of the Italian Alps with her, showing her the pretty villages. Any time she had free from her work in the Tyrolean holiday-home where she was looking after children, she was happy to spend with him. They seemed to dance together through these halcyon days, - weaving in and out of village streets, hand in hand, - sometimes he in his fawn barracks uniform and she in her pretty flowing print dresses. It was a time of happy relief from any responsibilities, - she had no teaching to do or husband to placate, and he often had extended leave-time which he could use for his enjoyment. The old ladies used to peep out of the windows as they frolicked by, saying "There go those two lovers again; let's hope they get married and live happy!"

They grew very close and affectionate, in a friendship sort of way, but she would never allow him to kiss her, or to come too close for emotional comfort. It was the one thing which spoilt something which would have been ideal as a romance.

"Are you playing a game with me?" he once asked, when he pulled her toward him, and she pulled away.

"No, no," said she, "it's not a game to me. It's just that I'm not ready, Gino, to get too close. . . No, not at the moment, not after what happened."

"Well what did happen?" He clasped her elbows, exasperated; "Something happened to you, my little English darling; and I want to know what it is!"

"I can't tell you!" And she broke away.

With that he had to be content.

I never explain what happened with Ewan! I just can't open up!

THREE

"Does it all have to be such a mystery?"

He asked this as they were travelling up a mountain in a funicular, with a wide fantastic view of mountains and valleys below them.

"A mystery?"

"Yes, it is such a mystery, what happened to you in Scotland, my little English darling! All you will tell me is that something did happen."

She held her hands over her face, not wanting to be directly challenged, standing opposite him, feeling distraught.

He went close to her, breathing over her, touching her chin sensitively and gazing into her eyes;

"You know you will never heal until you talk about it."

She gazed at a deep gorge of the valley below her and an endless vista of the mountains which stretched into a hazy distance. And then quite suddenly, as if struck with a heart-piercing sword, she clung to him, broke down and sobbed.

Yes, you are right; I need to tell my story; I can't continue like this. I need my heart to soften and be opened.

When they got to the top, Gino had to scoop her up from the floor where she lay collapsed in hysterics.

"Listen, I have an idea; come and visit my mother; she lives in Manarola, and we can go on a trip there. Though you can't tell it to me, maybe you will tell your story to her, and it will do you good."

"You suffer from a settled matter around your heart," - it was Gino's mother speaking, in her little house in Manarola, after giving them a luxurious Italian supper, - some matter which is making you miserable."

"Yes," chipped in Gino, "there's something wrong with her."

She smiled genially at Emily, ignoring her son.

She was quite an elderly lady, bowed with age, yet kind and pleasant in her face, with a mop of silvery-grey hair. Her eyes were bright, with crinkle-lines around them, which made her look so pleasant, combined with their youthful twinkle. When she smiled her whole face beamed.

"You and I must have a private conversation, - only for girls you know!"

Emily was willing to be led by her, away from Gino into a back-parlour which had a burning fire and slightly smoky smell.

"Now Emily," she said once they were seated, "you tell me all about it. . . How have you ended up with a broken heart? - Because that is what you have got, isn't it?"

Emily was about to protest, but the old lady with the youthful-looking eyes laid a hand on hers;

"You needn't confess to me that; I can tell a mile off! Or if it is not exactly broken, it is crushed. What I want to know is how you came by it!"

I can't tell her this; or can I ? She is kind and friendly and warm-hearted; I must trust to her, or have no help at all.

"Come on; trust me, and tell me your story; I am listening."

FOUR

Emily falteringly began to tell to the story of her Scotland adventure and grief;

"Well Ewan was wonderful at first. . . and I really loved him you see. . . and I was teaching these children. . . and he was gentle and chivalrous at first. . ." And she told the old lady her story, missing out nothing, ending with her escape from the house when he abused her.

The lady mused for a while; they sat next to each other in silence whilst the fire crackled in the grate.

"It seems to me Emily," the old lady suddenly spoke - "all you can do is that you must forgive him."

She reacted badly, almost angrily; "But why should I?"

"It's not a matter of why you should, it's not a matter of giving him what he deserves; but that without it, you cannot be free."

Free! Free? When have I not been free? Wasn't I free when I left him?

There was a long pause.

"Look at it this way," spoke the wisdom of old age; "you cannot be free of him, until the chains which bind you to him are released. And that is something only you can do."

Emily looked at her uncomprehendingly, so she tried another tack; "Have you ever considered why his behaviour toward you changed?"

"Well no, I haven't; he suddenly just didn't seem the same Ewan."

"Have you thought it might be his duties as a soldier which left him traumatized, which affected his mind and character?"

"What do you mean?"

"Well think! Had he seen active service just before the change came about? Many a soldier comes back traumatized after a battle you know, and behaves badly to his wife."

Oh really, is it common? Yet, now I come to think of it . . .

"Maybe if you had given him time to adjust, he may have become his old courteous self again."

"Are you telling me I shouldn't have run away when I did, or tried to escape from him? But I could no longer bear being under his fist."

The old lady pulled her chair closer and put her arm around the younger woman, all kindness and empathy.

"I'm not saying you shouldn't have brought the relationship to an end. I'm saying that if you can understand him and his situation better, it may help you to forgive him. Empathize, empathize, - that is the key."

The key is to empathize? Its meaning eluded her.

"It's the key to opening your heart, Emily, to enabling you to love again."

"*Oh!!*" Emily exclaimed this aloud, as if it struck home like a bolt of lightning.

"Because if you try to empathize, you will come closer to forgiving him, - and that will really set you free."

"And how will it set myself free, to let him off the hook?" She was now eager to learn the fullness of this ancient wisdom.

"Because your unforgivingness does not affect him, it enchains you. And your act of forgiveness lets loose those chains, - yes, cleaves them in twain!

Oh I begin to see!

A new dawn looked as though it was crossing Emily's face. She grasped the hand that lay on hers, and fiercely whispered,

"And how do I go about this?"

"Try to empathize, and then in your will make the act of just saying "I forgive him," and I can assure you, the release of your feelings will follow!"

Emily leapt up on the sudden as if she had a eureka moment.

Yes, Yes! She's told me everything I must do, everything in my life that I can ever do, - to be free, to be really free!

FIVE

It was very true that when Emily let go of what she held against Ewan, she found her own light-hearted happiness again, and was restored to her former self. She had tried out the old lady's wisdom, she had said "I forgive you Ewan" over and over many times, especially before going to sleep. And it actually worked its magic!

Then finally she got up one spring morning, opened the windows onto a spring scene, where the meadows were green and the birds singing, and it was gone; it was all gone, and dissolved away . . .

The poison in my heart is gone; it is forgiven; I am free.

She told Gino of course; she thanked him profusely for taking her to see his wise old mother; "She is really wise, you know, she's really wise!"

They were walking in Alpine meadows at the time, and he turned, presented to her some golden flowers he had been picking, and grinned broadly; "Yes, I know; my mother is wonderful, isn't she? Now. . . can we carry on from where we left off?"

"What on earth do you mean?" she asked, playfully hitting him.

"Well, you know. . . it was the kissing, if I remember."

"Alright, I give in."

They kissed long and deep, they rolled in the grass, they laughed in the sunlight. But Emily was cautious and careful;

I do not want things to rush ahead so quickly as they did with Ewan; for I think the speed was part of my mistake. I feel I still don't know Gino deeply enough.

"Let's go home, before we get too amorous!"

Emily's life soon seemed idyllic. In the course of a year Gino took her all over Italy to see the sights, and on the whole demanded nothing of her, beyond occasional kissing and embracing. He seemed content in her company, as she was in his; they were comfortable together, because their togetherness was based on genuine friendship and a shared sense of fun. She felt as happy, satisfied and fulfilled as she used to be a long time ago in Austria, fully restored as she seemed.

This friendship, or call it love of Gino, has such a happy brightness to it. He seems so generous and considerate. Yet I can't help sometime comparing him with Ewan, who was at first so kind and wonderful.

"Come on, my little English darling!" It was Gino, calling from the street below. "Hurry up, will you! What are you doing? We are going miss the train."

"I was just thinking; something about Scotland. . .but let's be off to Venice!"

I won't allow myself to consider what happened, for I seem restored, and as happy and free as I've ever been since Austria. I seem to be the same Emily again. It's wonderful how a heart can heal!

Emily did not foresee the dark shadow of what awaited her in Venice.

SIX

Emily was standing on the steps of San Marco, happily humming an Italian song which lingered in her head, whilst she waited for Gino. A group of Italian young men passed by and called after her "Bella," – she just smiled happily and gave a twirl in her stylish Italian skirts.

My past is behind me now; I feel perfectly content.

On Gino's arrival, they went in and explored the basilica; Emily was impressed by the paintings and statues, which seemed other-worldly and timeless. By the altar they stood and looked into each other's eyes, smiling trustfully.

"You are such a beautiful woman, Emily, and I know I have fallen in love with you. I have something to ask you."

"You have been so kind to me," she replied, trusting him utterly. But suddenly the thought of Ewan intruded into her head, and the fact that Gino did not actually know she was already married.

Though my heart is free, I'm not legally free; what on earth do I say if he's thinking of proposing?

Uncomfortable in the moment, she diverted his attention and pointed out some stunning paintings.

He mumbled distractedly; "It's not hard to be kind to a woman like you, my little English darling." And so the moment passed.

But it left Emily pondering for the rest of the day as regards his intentions, for their friendship was starting to take a more serious turn. They were happy for so long in this halcyon period of just enjoying each other's friendship and company, but it seemed to be coming to an end.

Why does this now happen? If he has to become serious, I will have to confess to him about Ewan, and all the trauma of that. Why does something so idyllic have to end? But I fear it will.

That evening as the full moon rose they took a gondola trip on one of the canals which shimmered with reflections from all the lights. He was looking at her intently and wistfully.

"Again I say, you are a beautiful woman, and I've fallen in love with you."

There was a long pause, as he waited for some kind of response.

"I believe I love you too Gino, but I can't do this, I just can't do this." And she buried her face in her hands.

He stretched out his hands to her, imploringly; "But I love you, and want to spend the rest the rest of my life with you. I love you, my beautiful Emily!"

"I'm not your Emily; I'm somebody else's Emily!"

But he never asked her what she meant by it. Instead, he moved to get close to her; snuggled close and started caressing her. Then he got more rough and pressed hard upon her. Suddenly she wasn't enjoying it anymore and it seemed a liberty.

"Gino, get off me!"

But he didn't stop, overwhelmed with real passion. With a triumphant look on his face, he forcibly pinned her down.

And in the rocking boat, tossing treacherously now on waters which had been calm, he overcame her . . .

SEVEN

Once indoors, packing hastily with the intention of leaving both Gino and Venice, she took no heed of Gino imploringly stretching out his hands, saying how sorry he was. For looking back at that moment when the silence had been palpable, it was as if a chasm had opened between them; and as if a figure climbed out of that chasm, - a black and wretched twisted figure of hatred and mistrust. And it would stalk them ever after, destroying all possibility of trust and friendship.

"Is that what you had in mind, bringing me to Venice? Mm? Answer me that!"

Gino hung his head, perceiving that he was going to get no allowance of forgiveness, and no trust from her ever again.

I feel I hate him now, as much as I ever loved him; how he has misused me! It's no good him being sorry now!

And her bitter rant went on, as she packed;

"Don't tell me you took me to see your mother, just to get your will of me, and with no care of me at all! And I thought at the time you wanted to heal my hurt heart, and was thinking of my good!"

She was handling a treasured and breakable ornament she had brought back from the Austria of her youth, and violently flung it at his head. It narrowly missed, and smashed itself to smithereens against the wall.

"That's what I think of you!"

"Wanted to heal my hurt heart" indeed! All you wanted was my body!

She was outside now, in the dark with her suitcase, and she found herself shouting it; "All you wanted from me was my body!"

Her voice passed over the canals of Venice, interlaced itself among the porticos, and passed out into the dark and gloomy night air.

At least Ewan wanted more than that; he wanted all of me.

She thought of the lean and hungry Ewan, like a wild wolf or bear hunting her, wanting ever more.

She kept walking, possessed of a strange preternatural energy. She began to wonder if she were going mad, because everything in the story of her life seemed to loom large in a frightening way.

After a long while, realising she had passed out of the city, instead of heading for the station as intended, she sank down on a stone, an old form of way-marker.

"Where am I going?"

She seemed to have been walking in a nightmare, or in a dream, or half asleep. It was the middle of the night, and she was dragging a suitcase along with great energy and speed to absolutely nowhere!

Yes, where am I going? To what idea, or ideal, or place on planet earth? I've no concept in my head at all of where I'm headed. When I was young, I knew I was headed to Austria, "Sound of Music" and all that! I can't now go back to Yorkshire; I'd feel too ashamed. I have nothing to guide me; I'm rudderless!

She inspected the old stone for a moment, but it gave her no clue. She hummed, singing to herself snatches of remembered songs, as she rocked herself in her dereliction of lonely grief.

"Greece, I'll go to Greece!" She raised her forefinger as the thought suddenly fell into her mind.

She had sought an answer in the sky, and the sky had whispered it back to her.

PART 3

Greece

ONE

THE BOAT, LOOKING small and vulnerable, was bobbing violently in turbulent water. He stood firmly on its deck, looking strong like a colossus, his chiselled fine Greek features creasing against the sun and dark locks flowing in the stiff breeze.

She looked down at him from the little quay, suspended in the moment, having been wandering aimlessly among thoughts of Ewan, so far-away and lost-to-her. . .

"What did you say?"

A hand was extended towards her, palm upward, -

"Do you trust me?"

She was surprised out of herself by the question; she perused his face, which was rugged and brown, yet generous and kind. Her dainty school-mistress hand went out to grasp his, rough, calloused and strong.

"Yes, I think so."

A warm grin broke upon him, lighting up his generous-looking countenance, - "Then come aboard my boat."

They were whisking across the blue Aegean, the sail hoisted and swelling before the wind, which turned all the water-troughs into white and frothed sea-foam, and churned it all back into the blue unseeing depths.

This is the first time I have ever been in a small boat on the sea before; the world of water seems so large, and I so small. It's romantic, it's wild!

"So what's your name Miss?"

His English was quite good, though marked with a strong Greek lilt; it made his speech seem like sing-song in the swaying atmosphere.

"My name is Emily."

My name has never sounded like this before, so small and delicate, so limited and fragile.

"I read a book by someone called Emily once. Now who was it? . ."

He had to yell above the noise of the flapping sails and sea-spray - "It was something about the Moors."

Emily nearly fell off her seat! The gurgling of the water reminded her to hold on, as she yelled into the wind, -

"You don't mean Emily Bronte! You don't mean Wuthering Heights!"

What's the chances of that! I leave the Yorkshire Moors, my favourite Emily Bronte country, I have all these adventures and come all this way, going through all these different countries, and meet a Greek guy on a boat who has read a book about the same place I originate from! That is unbelievable!

"Yeah, that's it," came the laconic reply.

Impulsive as ever, - for she had not lost that from her young nature,- she leapt up and hugged him, wrapping the force of her arms around his strong muscular form, though she barely reached his shoulders.

"Steady on! You'll have us collapsed and down there in a watery grave!" - The boat was rocking fearfully. - "Go back over there, there's a good girl, and resume your seat."

She sat down, stunned and in a strange reverie over her Yorkshire origins and the journey of her life thus far. He started to hum, then to whistle, and then to sing.

It seems a sad, wild Greek song, a song of the sea . . . or is it a song of love?

TWO

There came a knock on the door whilst she was eating her breakfast, in the small white-washed house on a hillside overlooking the bay.

I'm happy just looking across the sea right now, at its bright, sparkling, tempting waters.

"It's a man to see you Miss"- said her Greek landlady in broken English.

"Oh, who could that be?"

I know in my secret heart it's the man I've just been dreaming of, - the wild, handsome Greek boatman who has the look of the sea-god.

"Tell him to come in." And she hurriedly pinched her cheeks and smoothed her hair, feeling flustered.

"Here you are! I find you as pretty as an English rose-garden on this fine morning, Miss Emily. I have something for you."

And he brought a posy of sweet meadow-flowers from behind his back.

"Oh Stavros, that is very kind!"

Her mind flitted to when Ewan had first presented her with flowers in the schoolhouse; and later Gino had done the same. She flushed with an overload of memories and feelings.

"Why are you blushing?"

"Oh nothing, no reason," she deftly lied, motioning him to sit at the table.

Her mind flitted to a longing; to be lying on the couch with him, kissed all over. But she resisted it, and said in a bright voice;

"We should go out on the bright sea in your little boat, with birds of the air and fish of the deep all dancing around us, as the sun in the sky warms and cheers us."

"That sounds very poetic, Emily; do you really want to do that?"

"Yes, yes," she responded brightly, "that's what I want to do!"

"Then take my arm, my Emily, and I'll lead you along the streets to the quayside, where I've left my boat bobbing gently up and down, so that all the Greek fishermen can look out and be jealous of me."

"No Stavros, it is that all the Greek ladies can look out of their windows and be jealous of me!"

"Any which way, we will make a fine couple, winding down the little streets!"

She looked up at him as he stood up from the table;

Wow, he looks so handsome, with his thick curled hair, piercing blue eyes and white teeth, and those crinkled laughter-lines! He looks so bronzed, weather-beaten, and so strong!

"You make me feel. . ."

She paused and he reached out a hand to her, - a rough, strong hand, - and she spoke her thought;

"You make me feel so wild and free."

THREE

They were nestled in his little boat together, about to put out into the water.

"Why did you hold out your hand to me that day Stavros and say "Trust me"?

"Is that what I said?"

He smiled knowingly, and laughed.

He is even more handsome when he laughs; light seems to scatter from his lucent eyes!

"Yes, you said "Trust me."

"I know I did, my English flower. Tell me, do I have a roguish look on my face at the moment?"

"You always do, Stavros! But tell me, what did you mean by it?"

He was now busying himself with the boat, trying to get underway, with a concentrated look on his face before he answered.

"Well. . . it was to reel you in."

"Reel me in?!"

He looked at her shocked face, and gazed at it in contemplative fashion.

"Well you know, you looked lost, you looked hurt, you looked. . .you looked as if you needed comforting. So I thought. . .I thought if I offered you myself in terms of trust. . ."

". . .That it would reel me in, like a fish caught on a hook?"

"Something like that!"

He glanced again at her flushed and angry face, and tried to make excuses;

"It's just a fishing term Emily, used by a good-hearted fisherman here; I didn't mean anything by saying that."

"But I'm not sure I want to be caught like a fish!"

"Oh forget it Emily! Here, hold this; it belongs to the fishing tackle; I just need to reach the other rope."

Finally they got going, and were skimming over sparkling water, helped by a strong breeze. But Emily was oblivious to its beauty because she felt deeply unhappy.

I don't want to be seen as an object to be caught like a fish!

He saw the sullenness written on her face, and penitently held out his hand.

"Please, come on now. . .All I meant was that I was offering something to tempt you to engage with me, to start something off. . . It's not really anything like catching a fish."

She felt mollified, and reflected on it for a bit.

"But why did you use the word "trust"?"

"Well it seemed to me. . . you were walking so sad and downcast, as if someone had broken your heart, broken your trust. Affairs of the heart are governed by trust you know."

That is certainly true, all of that is true. Ewan and Gino have both broken my trust and my heart.

"So I'm trying to mend the hurt, and your heart, you see."

She reached out and touched his hand which he had been holding out to her; he reached out both, and grasped hers.

"Do we come to an understanding?"

"Yes Stavros, we do. You are a good man; you were trying to save me because I looked lost."

I smile because someone cares for me enough to want to save me.

He grinned broadly, then threw back his head and laughed;

"Isn't that what Jesus was supposed to do? - Save the lost?"

"Yes, I suppose so; but many others can share in that ministry."

FOUR

As the days passed and the bright summer progressed, Emily was lulled into feeling secure with this strong Greek man during outings on the blue Aegean sea.

At first she felt precarious, both because of the boat in its tossing motion, and because the man was an unknown quantity. A sense of less than perfect trust reigned in her initially, but after his avowal that he desired to comfort her, "save her because she looked lost," she acquired a coming-on disposition.

He looks so rough and tough, yet he's a gentleman at heart, and really I feel safe with him.

No alarm bells rang in her head regarding her previous experiences with men, - how they can turn in an instant from gentle to vicious. For in actual fact he was wooing her with a particular end in mind.

One morning he appeared at her door, flowers in hand yet again;

"Good morning, darling Emily, and what a good day it promises to be. Can I take you to my favourite island? It's a good day for it, weather-wise."

She answered distractedly and unsuspectingly, as she took hold of the pretty pink flowers;

"Yes, I'd like that. Where is it and what's it called?"

Yet another romantic adventure; I'm having lots of them; my life is good! Gone are the memories of the past which seemed to strangle me. I'm happy these days, - happy-go-lucky!

"It's quite a way away, a few hours in my little boat, but the sea is placid this morning, the sun shining and the sky blue, - all the things you like!"

"Yes, let's!" she unsuspectingly replied.

She got ready eagerly, wearing a swimming costume under her warmer clothes, as he had promised "a lovely beach there," and packed a picnic hamper too.

As she had her hand on the door, her thought suddenly flitted to the moment she opened the door of the monastery in Austria, and to memories of Pater Leo, - which seemed a lifetime ago.

I wonder what he would think of me if he saw me now? - no longer young and innocent? Instead, I'm hungry for some knowing of human love.

A pang of guilt passed through her, like fear of an omen.

"What's the matter?" he asked.

She decided to bury the moment.

"Kiss me Stavros!"

He smiled, with what looked like a wild secret pleasure;

"I'll kiss you later."

FIVE

And so they set off, in his bobbing boat on the blue sea, which was calm and placid this morning, to his special "secret island." And Emily didn't suspect any intention of his, because she had grown to like and trust him. And she herself was full to the brim with secret desire and longing.

"I'm so glad I met you Stavros, or that you chose me to come on your boat. It's been one of the best things ever!"

He bent a benign and winning smile on her.

The water soon got rougher and choppier as they travelled out, until now he had to keep both hands on the tiller. She pulled her hair out of its clasp, so it went wild and flying in the wind.

I'm sure the time has come at last! If only he would kiss me! How I'd love to swoon in those arms!

She gazed at him, and her eyes spoke the thought.

"So how about that kiss you wanted?" he suddenly, eagerly asked.

He took a moment to secure the boat. Then he gazed deeply into her eyes, and sensitively caressed her hair, before he passionately sank a long deep kiss upon her parted mouth.

This is wild and sweet, and energy tingles all over me, to the tips of my hair! It is like electricity all over me!

"Stavros, I love you!" she cried into the elements.

He grinned broadly; "You like that?"

He suddenly let go of her, and sat to take the tiller again;

"We are almost here; look, there's my island over there. Well it's not actually "mine," but I call it mine if you see what I mean."

There was a strip of perfect golden sand, with an idyllic green behind it. Shortly after, they had anchored the boat, and Stavros had jumped in, to swim the short distance to shore. Emily hastily stripped to her costume and jumped in too.

They began playing and tumbling in the water, amid the waves which were surging to the beach. She laughed and giggled and enjoyed their frolicking in the lucent, blue Aegean sea.

Then all of a sudden he became stronger and rougher, and grabbed her from behind, so it took her breath away. She became alarmed;

"Stavros, what are you doing?"

A wildness seemed to pass over his face, making him look a different man.

"You are mine, don't you think? Because I've brought you out here in this beautiful boat."

"You can't buy me like that; I didn't consent to. . ."

"Didn't consent to what? You were attracted; you came in my boat to my island; you know you want this. . ."

He was holding her face down upon the sand in the shallow water, as the sea-surge sent spray all about her.

You don't own me; No, you can't have me!

Emily cried it out, but it was lost amid the crashing of the waves on the lonely island. A sudden surge came from her spirit as she thrashed to loosen his grasp.

And in that solitary place in the middle of the wild unforgiving sea, he violated her . . .

SIX

It was necessary for Emily to sit silently, stubborn and sullen, all the way back in the boat with Stavros, in order to get off the island.

How can I endure such humiliation?

"I don't want to set eyes on you ever again, - not ever, you understand!"

She spoke this red and angry, with a tear-stained face, as she stepped back off the boat. He looked sheepish and crestfallen, but she was like a tower of wrath.

"I'll get you into trouble for this!" were her last words.

After all the abuse I've taken at men's hands, I'm not taking this lying down! I'll get the law to pursue Stavros. "Justice for all womankind" - that's what I say!

"Yes, that's the man!"

Stavros was being led by a group of Greek constabulary into the police station.

"And what charge do you make against this man, Miss, er, Miss. . .What's your name again?"

"It's Emily. . .And I want you to punish him for what he did to me; he hurt me and did me wrong; I want justice!"

"And what exactly did he do? . ."

The sergeant looked over his glasses and peered at her;

"For what exactly do you want justice?"

"He raped me!"

"Come now, rape is a very strong word. You will need witnesses and evidence you know. . ."

"How can there be witnesses on a deserted island, and any evidence is long gone, - unless it be my hatred for this worthless specimen of humanity!"

There was a long pause with a shuffling of feet, as a general embarrassment filled the room. Stavros himself glanced aside under her withering gaze.

Slowly she began to lose her nerve in the silence. She looked at the kind weathered face of the man, with the wrinkles round his eyes and even now a sparkle in them, and her courage failed her, and she found herself wringing her fingers.

He looks as brave and strong as a Greek god; how could the charge stick?

"You are quite sure you said No to him?"

The question took her aback; "Well I didn't say Yes."

There was another pause and it seemed to her the three policemen were smiling and winking at each other, as if it were a joke.

The sergeant leaned forward at this desk, whilst the others made Stavros sit on a chair, like an arraigned prisoner;

"I put it to you, Miss, that not saying Yes is not the same as saying No!"

She revolved it in her mind as though it were a puzzle; *"a double negative makes a positive" mathematically, and legally "silence construes consent." So he's saying, "I put it to you, you did not say No."*

Frustrated by her silence, which seemed long, her questioner turned to the accused, who relaxed confidently in his chair.

"And what do you say to this? She claims you raped her, out there near that favourite island of yours; what do you have to say, Stavros?"

He smiled laconically and charmingly, shrugging at the same time;

"Well when a pretty English girl gets into the boat of a handsome Greek man, and they put off into the sea together, what are you to think? Or more importantly, what are you to expect?"

How am I to get justice when they are all men? It makes me angry!

SEVEN

After Stavros' clever remark, all four policemen nodded knowingly, in what seemed a very Greek fashion;

"You mean her consent was implicit, to use legal language?"

"Yes it was." His reply was firm, and seemed to finalize the argument.

"You see our dilemma Miss, er. . .I'm sorry, I'm no good at English names. . It was a deed, which you claim was a crime, happening out at sea, hidden, with no witnesses. How can we assess it, when it is only your word against his!"

"But, but. . ." protested Emily, flailing in her sense of brokenness and vulnerability, in her anguish at not being believed;

"I tell you. . ." Her voice trailed off.

"And here is Stavros," the sergeant went on, apparently assuming the role of both judge and jury with consummate ease, "Here he stands, a model villager in our community, always just, always kind, well-known and beloved by all, - and never" - here he jibed his finger at poor Emily,- " never in his life offending against the law! No, Miss Emily, you will find no friends among us, if you persist in this calumny."

Emily's head sank down in despair;

"Well, I guess I will have to withdraw my accusation."

I hoped to have justice, and have found none!

"Yes, withdraw it; that's the best thing you can do! I suggest, Ms Emily, that as the English saying goes, - "You made your bed, and then had to lie in it!"

She detected a sneer in his voice.

"Do you honestly not believe me?"

"Look at Stavros, just look at him; he is a fine specimen of Greek manhood; do you think he could be guilty of such a thing! Has it not occurred to you that he could readily acquire any Greek woman that he desired? Why should he pursue a little English girl like you, who would probably give little satisfaction?"

There was an undoubtable sneer in his voice this time. And she could hear the other policemen sniggering.

She stood up in a wretched state of misery, saying bitterly "Oh forget it!"

And she stalked out, trying to hold her head high.

As she passed, Stavros whispered at her - "I'll not forgive you for this!"

Once outside, she heard loud raucus laughter from all of them, as they told crude jokes at her expense.

Well, I'll pursue my way home-ward from here, feeling shame, only shame!

PART 4

Yorkshire

ONE

A GREAT DESPONDENCY SETTLED on Emily; she felt she had come to a dead end. Her sense of adventure, her love of life, was lost. She turned to go home, miserable and defeated.

It's back to those Yorkshire moors for me, which I left so long ago. What's the point of a sense of adventure anyway? You end up disillusioned and broken-hearted!

Travelling back from Greece was quick and easy enough, and without incident; she just remained cold and unresponsive. Entering her home-county of Yorkshire was a bit more difficult, for she felt uncertain of her welcome, rather diffident and anxious.

Suppose they don't welcome me? Suppose they are angry with me, just deserting them all those years ago, to pursue a fool's dream, - something that was "pie in the sky" and unreal to them? And yet I so much wanted at the time to go to Austria, and have experiences like Maria in "The Sound of Music"! I so wanted to be free of the dirt and grime of Yorkshire, and what I felt was the oppression of my family. And then I suppose I just kept on going, - pursuing love affairs which fulfilled my thirst for life and adventure. It's all come to a sad end I suppose!

She had sent a letter in advance of course to warn them of her coming, but as she waited at the small railway station to be picked up, she only felt how badly and thoughtlessly she had treated her family, her Aunt Bessie and Uncle Arthur, and she felt fearful at the prospect of entering their home again.

Are my Aunt and Uncle going to be angry with me? Are they going to understand that I had to go, and now equally I've had to come back for something like a refuge from the world?- that harsh cruel world where I've been so badly treated? Is there going to be any understanding between us?

Once she was shown indoors and put down her luggage, as soon as she saw Aunt Bessie she collapsed onto her neck and wept.

"Nay, what's all this!" said the bustling lady, "you just sit down and I'll make ye a nice cup o' tea."

Emily felt she had travelled a long way before returning, and had rather thrown herself on their hospitality.

I feel I'm more like a wandering stranger come in from the cold, than family!

Soon they were all sipping tea, feeling shy and self-conscious.

"So ye've come back to us, eh?" said Uncle Arthur, leaning back against that old familiar sideboard and lighting his pipe. He took a few puffs first before he went on, filling the room with an aroma of the tobacco which Emily had always loved;

"And did ye learn owt?"

She replied meekly and respectfully; "Yes Uncle, I learned a lot."

She thought of those moments with Ewan, Gino and Stavros, when she felt she could die of shame and sorrow, when some bottomless pit of cosmic horror had opened at her feet, and threatened to swallow her.

"Ah, but ye know what I mean; did ye learn owt that was worth the going away to learn?"

She gazed at him in his earnestness and fidgeted sadly on her seat. It was a tortuous question, and one which provided a sad insight into her soul's condition. She voiced her deepest thought;

"*No, Uncle, perhaps not, perhaps not!*"

TWO

Emily slowly settled into her new abode. Her Aunt let her stay in her old bedroom, ousting one of her two cousins, - and she now found these two children a diverting amusement to have around, and played games with them. She helped her Aunt Bessie to clean bedrooms, hang out washing, to cook and make scones and apple pies. It was humdrum, with nothing special happening, but its ordinariness suited her at the moment.

Okay, there is nothing beautiful or inspiring here, - no amazing scenery, no mountains, no young men to have romances with, but I've had enough of those things. I am content now with what I have, and ask for nothing more.

She started going for long walks with her Uncle, largely "in the gloaming," that evening hour when the light was just fading. They walked up through the housing estates, looking at all the flowers in the pretty gardens, until they reached the summit of the road from where they could espy the Moors stretching away in all their splendour, with the quiet glow of the evening illuminating their heights. At those times it felt good to Emily to be back, - she felt a sense of really being at home whilst gazing at her beloved Moors.

They usually walked arm in arm, like good comrades, - with a close affection which never existed between them before. She confided in him many things which she had encountered, - but whenever it got really emotional and personal, she stopped short, drawing a veil over things.

"Ye should tell your Aunt Bessie these stories," he said on one occasion, "They make for real adventures."

"Adventures end up with you getting hurt," she replied.

"Did you get hurt?"

"Yes, Uncle, I got very hurt!"

Time passed, and she started doing other things, as she felt more confident; going into town shopping for her Aunt, or on the bus for a trip to one of the big towns, - more importantly, walking further afield, putting on her hiking boots and climbing the Moors. Then once she climbed Ilkley Moor in the early morning, and got back before breakfast, like she used to do. And this was truly liberating, making her feel her old youthful self again, before all the ghastly things had started happening to her.

They may have seemed good at the time, but they were ghastly; because they sullied my brightness, like a stain on my soul. And now I begin to feel truly myself again, - me, essence of Emily!

It seemed strange to her almost that, after all her seeking of adventures in different countries, she began to feel content and at home in the Yorkshire where she grew up. She appreciated her family's closeness and company, the Yorkshire landscape, and the Moors which constantly stood over her and were as shepherds to her thoughts.

I can hardly understand now why I felt so driven to escape from Yorkshire; it had seemed so oppressive and stifling, but now it wraps me round with a sense of security and comfort,- like a balm to my wounded soul!

THREE

The faces of men, - her three lovers, Ewan, Gino, Stavros, - circulated around her and passed through her dreams; men who had maltreated her, abused her. She rejected all of them now with a sense of disgust.

If only I could win back that purity of soul I had in Austria; in my virgin-youth, when I only knew pure love!

She could remember vividly how she climbed those mountains with energy and brightness of soul, how she strode along confident and bold, how she felt she had the world at her feet. She remembered how she had met her monk-friend Pater Leo, how tenderly and shyly she related to him, how it sang her soul alive with sweetness. In comparison, all her other loves were so earthy and physical. She wanted them physical at the time, but now she felt sullied by that earthiness, by the dirt of them.

Pater Leo was right; a better path for me would have been to become a nun!

Having the monk so much in her thoughts, she started to write long and profuse letters to him again; he said in his replies that he was glad to hear from her again, and wondered why she had ceased contact when she was in Scotland. In her replies, she didn't confess the reason, because she felt a deep sense of guiltiness, - even though the guiltiness lay at someone else's door more than her own.

I feel more sinned against than sinning, but how deeply I feel my own sin! I am feeling shame I suppose; that I so willingly got involved with these men, who seemed to have one thing on their minds. But Oh, how I wish it had never happened! – that I had walked through that door and never found Ewan awaiting me on that desk, that I had never given way to this temptation to have illicit adventures! Why didn't I just keep on the narrow path!

And so she went on, involved in her tortuous thoughts, whilst on the surface she participated with her Aunt and Uncle and cousins in their humdrum Yorkshire life, smiling outwardly to them and not revealing how inwardly she felt miserable and ashamed.

She was lying on her bed one day, looking out at her favourite tree, the one that stood faithfully there since her childhood, like a witness to her growing up. She vividly remembered Ewan, how violent he got, then Gino, who took such a liberty, then Stavros, who lured and tricked her and walked away scot-free. She just recalled it all so vividly, probing that misery and shame;

It seems that's what men do, unless they vow celibacy, - they use and abuse women. Yes, how they use and abuse!

And she burst into tears, violent and unrestrained sobbing. Above all she felt sorry for herself, a genuine pity for her lost innocence.

I was a pure white canvas, now I'm a dirty old rag! Something beautiful could have been written on my soul, now I am sullied and of no good to anyone. I'm no good! And I can come to no good.

So she reflected on her experience, and thought and tormented herself, not looking on anything forgivingly. . . until she met Peter.

FOUR

Here she sat on the heights of Ilkley Moor again, that beloved place form which she had launched her life. It was at this spot that she had that original fall, and met that strange elderly man who had persuaded her to follow her dreams and make "the Sound of Music" a reality for herself. She had always experienced it as a place to ponder and think. She pondered deeply now, weighing her experiences against her loss of innocence. Again the faces of her lovers swirled around her, - as she attempted to become more forgiving, both to them and herself.

Gino didn't really just want me for my body, did he? We had been best friends before he had even kissed me. It wasn't true, what I shouted that night.

She saw before her his handsome friendly face and attractive manner, dressed in his uniform.

And Stavros didn't really rape me, in the way I had launched that accusation. I had desired it and caused it myself.

She thought of his sunburnt face and laughter lines around his eyes, as he stood proudly on his boat, buffeted by wind and tossed on Greek seas. She felt the pull of attraction even now.

As for Ewan, I don't know what was going on with him. But he did at first tenderly and nobly love me and sweetly desire to marry me. I think really it was his fighting life which made his connection with me deteriorate, and he couldn't handle his own strength.

She had an image of him dressed in his highland garb, his manly strength. She remembered his sweetness at the lochside when she had offered "all of herself."

All of these thoughts made her sad. She stood up and shook herself, looking down at the town below. She walked up and down trying to get to the essence of some clue; she felt there was a mistake she had kept repeating;

All wanted something from me. Yet none of them really knew me.

They all knew her carnally, but stopped short of understanding her soul.

Her mind flicked to her "first love," the monk who was her "soul-friend," Pater Leo. A rush of affection for him entered her, as she realised how faithfully he had waited whilst she was having her "romantic adventures," just wondering what was occupying her, plying her with reminders that he was "there for her." She was impatient of it at the time, but now it seemed a magnificent kindness.

He knew me, he knew me all along. But I can't tell him about this, no, I can't ever tell him of my romantic adventures, because he knew me in my innocence. Or maybe I can, maybe I should. . . He might find me a way of forgiving it all, including myself for my mistakes.

Then there was Peter, the staid and true Yorkshireman whom she had recently met, introduced by her Aunt. He was not a wild or handsome or romantic man, it is true, but she'd had enough of those. He was genuine and kind, honest and homely, gentle and courteous, and Emily liked him.

He asks nothing of me; he just lets me be myself, - me, Emily. Yes, he just lets me be . . .

FIVE

Emily lay in bed in the darkness, feeling solitary on Christmas Eve, though she could hear her family downstairs, whilst wind and rain beat mercilessly against her window-pane.

Will it turn to snow? Will it snow to give us a white Christmas?

She snuggled deeply under the covers, but sleep eluded her. Then as so often, the faces of Ewan, Gino, Stavros, swam in a vague mist in her half-dozing state. She found she felt angry as well as sorrowful;

You took my dreams from me!

And she burst into tears.

The tears seemed to alleviate her intense feelings, but still the faces hovered over her, and she examined them one by one. – Ewan, who seemed to love her intensely but ended up abusing her; Gino. who seemed to take her for a ride with a view to the one thing he wanted; Stavros, whose sole purpose in charming her seemed rapacious.

You all robbed me of my innocence. Where has Emily gone? What's now left of me?

Suddenly in this wide bewildering grief, a memory intruded, - a memory that was sharp, strong and incisive. It was that of Gino's mother, saying in that lovely old house in Manarola;

"Your unforgivingness doesn't affect them, it enchains you. And your act of forgiveness lets loose those chains."

It cut deep, and completely woke her to clear consciousness.

Of course, I can't be free, until the chains which bind me to them are released! She said it was the key to opening my heart to love again. And to forgive, I just make the act of will, and the feelings will follow.

"Just say it Emily! Just make an act of the will!"

She summoned each of their faces in turn; "I forgive you. . .and you. . .and you. . . I forgive you all."

As the rain outside turned to floating snow-flakes, she remembered what she had afterwards shouted; "Your mother has told me everything I can ever do in my life to be really free!"

And she fell happily into an exhausted sleep.

The first thing she did on waking in the morning was to look out at the thick whiteness which deeply coated everything, and hung bright and tantalizing on all the tree branches and twigs.

Everything looks pure and white and virginal! And yes, I feel lighter, brighter, relieved and restored!

As she hurried to go downstairs, - where her uncle was playing the Christmas music, which always signalled to them the start of this celebratory day, - it struck her what Christmas was all about, - a mother giving birth to a baby.

It's one of the deepest meanings of life, - maybe I've been barking up the wrong tree, and searching for the wrong thing.

It struck her that seeking for sexual fulfilment, and not motherhood, may have been where she came unstuck.

"It's just a thought," she murmured, "just a thought."

SIX

But that thought took root that day, on Christmas morning, and it grew and filled her with a new concept and purpose during the following year's passing. Gradually, having made her act of forgiveness, the torment in which she had mentally allowed herself to stew since her return to Yorkshire, just got washed away from her more and more. It was true indeed that feelings of release did follow; soon she found thoughts of her past lovers no longer occupied her at all. It was as if each day brought a successive wave to cleanse the beach which was her consciousness.

She felt even more released because, once she had confessed the tale of that brief and sad, violent marriage to her uncle, he said it would be no problem given those circumstances to get a divorce. Emily was grateful to him that he helped arrange it for her, so then she felt even more free of her past.

One morning in Spring, when she was happy amidst the green world of the daffodils, she suddenly realised that all memory of the past pain associated with her lovers, was entirely gone. She could remember their faces by an act of memory, but they no longer haunted her, and were no longer wedded to pain. She felt indeed free and happy.

And she had so many things to engage her mind and soul, as the screwed-up part of her began to stretch and breathe and blossom again. She was in deep communion with Pater Leo again, still faithfully there for her, sending a constant flurry of letters. There was a dear family whom she quickly grew so fond of, feeling they were kin to her, being like her in so many ways. There was the wonder of all those moors to explore, in all their different seasons. And there was dear Peter, so staid and true, so kind and attentive; she held a hope that they might be married.

And this time I will wait till I'm married to give my all to him, and I will be hoping to bear his child.

She wrote a lot about this very thing to Pater Leo, - she told all her feelings about Peter, when of course she had concealed the truth about her former partners. This she realised was probably that deep-down she knew them to be mistakes, - immoral relationships that "missed the mark" of what true love should be. She told Pater Leo all about that miraculous experience of Christmas Eve, when she made an act to forgive her lovers, how forgiveness had set her free as that wonderful old lady had told her it would. She also started to tell him a lot about those experiences when she vigorously pursued her love-adventures. He gently suggested to her that pursuing adventures to gain sexual experiences was a mistake. In one letter he said to her outright that love should not be a "wild adventure," but a growing union of two people whose love will hopefully be fruitful.

Ah, I see now!

Emily put down the letter, which moved her to gentle, sweet tears.

I see I was always making the same mistake! I was willing to do anything for the sake of wild adventure, and it led me to have sexual relationships which were what could be called illicit, immoral. It is mistakes that make us human, but that was an awfully big mistake!

She thought some more, cried some more, then pronounced;

I can forgive myself now! Yes, I think I can forgive myself!

SEVEN

So I've forgiven them, and forgiven myself, and everything is good and I am completely myself again!

Thus was Emily's thought on the succeeding Christmas Eve.

"As for Peter. . ." A smile came to her lips at the sweetness of her feelings.

No, that wouldn't be a wild adventure; there is something lasting and solid about it. And I like that we have agreed not to come together until our wedding night.

She pondered as she gazed at the familiar scene out of her bedroom window, before starting to write her journal, - a new practise of hers encouraged by Pater Leo.

She wrote of how she loved the Yorkshire Moors; how she now yearned for life with a similar lasting, solid quality, She realised that all her wild escapades were connected with the fluidity of water, happening by or in water; now she felt grateful to be surrounded by something more solid, - the roots of the Moors thrusting into Yorkshire soil.

She vividly recalled in her writing the last Christmas Eve, when she had finally begun to properly heal by that act of forgiveness,- recalling each of her lover's faces and saying "I forgive you." And how she awoke in the morning to a blanket of pristine snow and felt bright and restored. Yes, it was that act of forgiveness that night which had set her free from the demons of the past haunting her.

Then she called to mind that "thought" which had surprised her on Christmas morning, - that the deepest meaning of life was what Christmas was all about, - a mother giving birth to a baby. After a year of slowly mulling this over, she wrote something which surprised her;

"I'd like to be a mother; that would be a life with a solid, lasting quality. I'm sure it would fulfil me, create me. . . into the Emily I am meant to be."

She looked at what she had written, and realised that indeed she really was yearning to be a mother. She carried on writing that she was going to lay aside her craving for "wild adventures." She had learned this year to have a right appreciation of the whole of a relationship, and not just her own sexual fulfilment, to value a man who was willing to work and support her, grow to maturity and bring up a child with her. She was thinking of Peter of course; all her desires circulated around him.

"I do so hope he will soon propose!" - were her last words before she put down the pen.

And at the turning of the year, on a blue-skied first day of January, when plentiful snow covered Emily's beloved Moors, Peter did indeed ask her to become his wife. He got on his knee with deep sincerity, Emily blushed and spoke her "Yes" from the core of her being, and it was good news which her family applauded.

Emily felt wrapped in genuine love, and she knew Peter and the children they might have would fulfil her, and give her all that she desired in life. She knew she truly loved him because she desired his child.

And so they were married, in Yorkshire in 1986. And she settled down and lived happily ever after.

Yes me, Emily! - Content at last!